*Corporate Insights*
2111 Plum St., Ste 250
Aurora, IL 60506

I0663766

*Praise for*
# The Four Factors of Effective Leadership

David Rendall has done a **SUPERB** job of offering up a straightforward, useful, and *enjoyable* framework for understanding the often complex and too often overcomplicated nature of leadership. *The 4 Factors of Effective Leadership* integrates the research and writing of the outstanding scholars in the field and then offers readers the essentials, gives us a way to assess our current competence in each, and points us in the direction of improvement. It's **a great place to start your leadership journey**.

- Jim Kouzes
*Coauthor of the bestselling book, **The Leadership Challenge***

As we move from the Information Age into the Conceptual Age, creative leadership is becoming essential -- for professional success, personal fulfillment, and community well-being. This **SMART, INSPIRING** work -- *a symphony of timeless leadership principles* -- can be your guide. Leaders of every kind would do well to **read this book and heed its lessons**.

- Daniel H. Pink
*Author of **A Whole New Mind** and **Free Agent Nation***

David Rendall has done all aspiring leaders a big service. He has condensed the best research on leadership and personal effectiveness into a short, **FASCINATING**, and *useful* guide that can launch you down the path of helping others to attain their greatest impact in work and life.

- Tom Morris
*Author of such books as **True Success** and **If Aristotle Ran General Motors***

*The 4 Factors* does a **MASTERFUL** job of synthesizing the best concepts in leadership development and adding something *unique* and worthwhile to them. The 'Factor Quotient' sections alone contain a **priceless** pearl: Leaders should endeavor to maximize their effectiveness in their areas of greatest strength.

- Stosh D. Walsh
*Strengths Consultant/Seminar Leader, **The Gallup Organization***

David Rendall's book is a must for anyone desiring to understand the fundamentals of leadership. His skillful inclusion of *inspirational* quotes and **practical** applications make this book unique.

- J. Douglas Hood, MBA
*Former Director of Operations, **Flowers Industries***

I enjoyed the book's synthesis of the leadership literature and the use of simple constructs. I really like the concept that leaders need to be able to lead themselves before they can lead others. The insights in this book will be *helpful* in my work with leaders and coaches.

- Curt Liesveld
*Co-Author of Living Your Strengths*
*Senior Strengths Consultant,* **The Gallup Organization**

This is a book that everyone can understand. It is a condensed version of leadership principles that you will enjoy reading. It is practical and serves as an **EXCELLENT** model. Regardless of your occupation, I highly recommend this book.

- Dave Hill, Ed. D
*Former Director of Operations,* **Sam's Club Brazil**

Rendall's *insightful* use of metaphor makes **clear** the basic characteristics required for leadership and the fact that anyone who wishes to be a leader can become one.

- Nancy Holley, Ph. D.
*Principal Consultant,* **Computer Sciences Corporation**
*Adjunct Faculty,* **Fielding Graduate University**

This book offers an easy to understand and *practical* leadership model. These factors will truly result in effective leadership.

- Michael Lowstetter
*Vice-President of Finance,* **Shepherds, Inc.**

David's book brought **focus** to my leadership. His principles are not only effective, they are also right. I highly recommend this book to anyone who desires to take their leadership to new heights.

- Jonathan Misirian, M. Div.
*Senior Pastor,* **Southbrook Church**

The Four Factors will encourage aspiring leaders and also challenge those with many years of leadership experience.

- Susan Ford
*Educator and Lecturer*

## *Other Resources By David Rendall*

GROW! Ten Strategies for Maximizing your Leadership Potential
- Live Seminar Audio CD or mp3
- Live Seminar DVD

CREATE! Leading by Initiating Change and Inventing the Future
- Live Seminar Audio CD or mp3
- Live Seminar DVD

RECHARGE! Avoiding Burnout through Personal Renewal
- Teleconference Seminar Audio CD or mp3

THE FOUR FACTORS OF EFFECTIVE LEADERSHIP
- Live Seminar Audio CD or mp3
- Live Seminar DVD

## Coming Soon!

THE FOUR FACTORS OF EFFECTIVE LEADERSHIP
- Unabridged Audio Book (Winter 2006)

THE FREAK FACTOR: Discover and Develop Your Hidden Strengths
- Book (Summer 2007)

* to order, please visit www.drendall.com

**F4ctors of Effective Leadership**

Keep away from people that belittle your ambitions.
Small people always do that, but the truly great make you feel that
you too can become great.

*- Mark Twain*

To order additional copies, please contact us.
BookSurge, LLC
www.booksurge.com
1-866-308-6235
orders@booksurge.com

# F4ctors of Effective Leadership

*Revised & Updated*

David J. Rendall

**BookSurge, LLC**
North Charleston, South Carolina

# Acknowledgements

This book would not have been possible without the love and support of many people. My wife, Stephanie, and my daughters, Anna Marion and Emma Grace, provided me with inspiration. I owe any success that I achieve to the selfless love and leadership of my parents.

Susan Ford, Nancy Holley, Jonathan Misirian and Vernon Rendall patiently reviewed drafts of this book as it was being developed. Tom Morris, Curt Liesveld and Stosh Walsh provided helpful feedback for this revised edition. Their insights were invaluable. Michael Lowstetter developed the factor quotient assessments and designed the four factors logo.

I owe my passion for leadership to Elliott Anderson, who taught me how to lead and to Norm Hoyt, who introduced me to ideas and experiences that changed my life. I am similarly indebted to Warren Anderson for any writing skills that I possess.

# Dedication

To my mother and father, whose lives exemplify the four factors

# Contents

*Preface*      *1*

**Introduction**      **4**

**Inside-Out**      **12**

**Factor 1: Influence**      **29**
- Internal:      Self-Discipline
- Interpersonal:      Influence
- Factor Figure:      Mahatma Gandhi
- Factor Failure:      Jim Jones
- Factor Fiction:      Power

**Factor 2: Integrity**      **51**
- Internal:      Credibility
- Interpersonal:      Trust
- Factor Figure:      Abraham Lincoln
- Factor Failure:      Hitler
- Factor Fiction:      Personality

**Factor 3: Inspiration**      **70**
- Internal:      Personal Mission
- Interpersonal:      Shared Vision
- Factor Figure:      Dr. Martin Luther King Jr.
- Factor Failure:      Josef Stalin
- Factor Fiction:      Position

**Factor 4: Improvement**      **95**
- Internal:      Self-Development
- Interpersonal:      Developing Others
- Factor Figure:      Jack Welch
- Factor Failure:      "Chainsaw" Al Dunlap
- Factor Fiction:      Popularity

**Impact**      **122**

*About the Author*      *129*

*References*      *130*

# Preface

I was recently interviewed by a local reporter. She began our discussion by explaining that she had already had all the information that she needed for the story. My press release, overview and book reviews had answered all of her questions. Now, she said, she wanted to talk about the heart and soul behind the book. She wanted to go deeper. She asked, "Why did you write this book?"

It was a good question, and I'm embarrassed to admit that, until that moment, it was one that I hadn't consciously considered, but it didn't take me long to find the answer. It wasn't far from my mind and as I shared my thoughts with her, I realized that it was a very important question with a meaningful answer. In this revised edition of the book, I want to share my heart with you.

The story of this book began on New Year's Eve more than 15 years ago. I was with a large group of high school friends and we'd been playing outside in the cold snow of a Wisconsin winter. When we came in the house, we received news that one of our friends had been shot in a hunting accident. His name was Kyle Wilson and he died later that morning. We were stunned. The news was even more shocking because another one of our friends was responsible for the shooting. We all went to a small private school and everyone knew each other, but no one knew Kyle like I did.

Kyle and I weren't just friends. We were best friends, lifelong friends. I was born in October and he was born in November of the same year. Our parents knew each other from church and I don't really remember a life before Kyle. We had gone to the same schools since kindergarten. This was significant because I went to five different schools between kindergarten and high school. Kyle's family always changed schools when mine did. Since we also went to church together every week, there was barely a day that we didn't see each other. My frequent moves from school to school meant that I kept leaving other friends behind. Kyle was one of the few people that I really felt comfortable with. He was one of the few people who really knew me.

When Kyle died, I was devastated, but I quickly realized that I wasn't the only one in pain. He was dating a girl at the time of his death and she received a letter from him the day after his death. She had a difficult family situation and Kyle had been one of the bright spots in her life. Then there was the boy who shot Kyle, I still can't imagine how he must have felt. Watching these people grieve and suffer created a desire to help, to ease their pain.

I spent a lot of time listening to my friends as their worked through their sense of loss. During this time, I discovered two things. First, there were a lot of people in the world who were in pain and needed help. Second, I could help. I had something to offer. I realized how fortunate I was. I realized that I had been blessed with a great family and a lot of wonderful opportunities. Prior to this time, I hadn't experienced a lot of major difficulties in my life. This wasn't true for everyone and I made it my goal to do whatever I could to help others. Before Kyle's death, I didn't really have a purpose for my life. Now I did. My mission was to help others.

To fulfill this mission, I studied psychology in college and my first job after graduation was helping students in special education find internships and job training. As I continued working in the nonprofit sector, I was disappointed by the lack of leadership. I met a lot of people who, like me, wanted to help others. Unfortunately, poor management, politics, ineffective organizational systems and a lack of clear direction left most people disillusioned or burned out. It occurred to me that the way to really help people was to improve the leadership of the nonprofit sector. Someone needed to help those who helped others. My new mission was to help those who were trying to make a difference in the world.

My career quickly began to include greater and greater levels of management responsibility. I started as a coordinator of a small program with two part time employees. Within five years I was managing twenty-five people at a large nonprofit organization. By the end of ten years, I was a senior executive, responsible for leading more than 75% of the organization's employees. These experiences, and the many challenges involved, helped me to learn more about leadership than I could ever get from books. However, it also showed me the wisdom of much that I'd read.

My current work as a professor, trainer and consultant gives me almost unlimited opportunities to contribute to the lives of others. In my new career I try share ideas that will inspire people to reach their potential so that they, in turn, will use their success to improve the lives of others. This book is an extension of that work. I have been inspired many of the books that I have read. I hope that this book will inspire you to become a more effective leader and that you will use what you learn to make a positive difference, to make the world a better place. There are a lot of people in this world that are hurting. You can help.

David Rendall
Goldsboro, North Carolina
June 6, 2006

# Introduction

If we are to improve our understanding and practice of leadership, we must first agree on what leadership is. In other words, we must define leadership.

– Mike DeGrosky        CEO, *Guidance Group*

## A Tale of Two Leaders

In 1933, Adolph Hitler began a reign of terror that ravaged Europe for the next twelve years. He caused the deaths of millions of Jews, as well as German soldiers and citizens during World War II. At one point, German forces controlled most of Europe and parts of Northern Africa, but following D-Day in June 1944, Allied troops gradually eroded the German stranglehold. As Hitler's success turned to failure, he hid deep in a bunker complex near the heart of Berlin. When it became clear that there was no hope for escape, he killed himself and his wife and left instructions for their bodies to be burned.

Hitler's time in power was marked by fear and deception. He fostered violent hate and deep mistrust among the German people. According to historian Robert Wistrich, Hitler used "propaganda, terror and intimidation to secure his hold on power." He was an incompetent military strategist and his overwhelming ambition led him to invade Russia before he had control of England. This decision made it virtually impossible for Germany to win the war. Some historians also believe that Hitler may have been mentally ill.

Hitler envisioned a world that was dominated by a pure Aryan race and in which all inferior people, including Jews and those with disabilities, had been exterminated. The German people were led astray by his masterful use of deceit and manipulation. As a result, their country was destroyed and their fathers, husbands, and sons were slaughtered. In the end, Hitler demonstrated an inability to control himself, influence his people, or create the *perfect world* that he imagined.

In 1869, Mohandas Gandhi was born into a country that was oppressed by imperialistic power and prejudice. For nearly 100 years, the

British ruled India to various degrees, while Indian political leaders focused on their self-interest, instead of the welfare of the Indian people. In contrast, Gandhi led through a strategy of hope and empowerment. He encouraged love and trust and demonstrated incredible self-sacrifice. The people of India were poor and uneducated, but because of Gandhi's leadership, the Indian people learned that they could govern themselves, earn a living, and control their destiny. His efforts eventually secured the freedom of more than 300 million Indian citizens and brought independence to one of the largest countries in the world.

Both the British and Indian people were deeply influenced by his words and actions. As a sign of deep respect, he was given the title *Mahatma*, which means "great soul." Biographer B. R. Nanda remembered Gandhi as "a man who schooled himself in self-discipline, made his life a continual process of growth, and tenaciously adhered to certain values to which humanity pays lip-service while flouting them in practice." Shortly after the British granted independence to India in 1947, Gandhi was assassinated by a Hindu fanatic. During his life, he demonstrated an incredible ability to control himself, influence others, and make positive changes in the world around him.

### Asking Questions

*Who was the greatest leader in the history of the world?*
    This is the question that I ask participants in my leadership classes and seminars. Despite the incredible differences between the leadership of Hitler and Gandhi, they are chosen by nearly every group. People also choose religious and political leaders, as well as celebrities, parents, teachers, and coaches. Even though some routinely make the list, there is certainly no clear consensus regarding the greatest leader. That leads to the next question.

*Why do you think these people were great leaders?*
    The answers to this question help explain why people cannot agree on a single greatest leader. As with the first question, few answers stand out. Charisma, communication, intelligence, success, and other reasons are given. People choose great leaders based on personal ideas of what leadership is, but most participants seem to be working with different theories of leadership. They cannot agree on the definition of leadership, much less anything beyond that.

*What is leadership?*

Maybe students and leadership seminar participants are not the people to ask. Maybe I should ask the experts. Warren Bennis, professor and well-known author on the subject of leadership, says that "leadership is like beauty; it's hard to define, but you know it when you see it." Is that true? Do people really know it when they see it? If so, then why is there such disagreement about who the great leaders are? If Hitler and Gandhi were great leaders, what does that mean about leadership?

## Searching for Answers

As a young manager of a nonprofit organization, I wanted answers to these questions. I wanted to know how to become an effective leader. I wanted to understand what to do and how to do it. So, I read. I found every book that I could on the subject of leadership and read them, book after book after book. The problem was that I did not know exactly which books to read. I just moved from one to another based on my own interests and recommendations from others.

To get a more comprehensive understanding of the subject, I began working on my doctorate in management and organizational leadership. I thought this would provide the answers that I needed. The program included four classes on leadership theory. The most promising course required a 1000+ page text, *Bass & Stogdill's Handbook of Leadership*, which weighed about ten pounds and attempted to assemble all of the writings and research on leadership since the beginning of time. The book actually began with an explanation of some Egyptian hieroglyphics. However, I was quickly disappointed as I read more than fifteen pages devoted to competing definitions of leadership. The authors concluded that there was no common definition of leadership, although they did propose their own. Needless to say, this was not much of a foundation for my leadership career.

The lack of clarity in the field of leadership extended far beyond disagreements regarding definitions. For example, one of the classic unresolved questions is whether leaders are born or made. Some people believe that leadership is a magical phenomenon that simply cannot be explained, taught, or learned. This idea is most often related to the idea of charisma. Many assume that charismatic leaders have a magnetic quality, which draws people to them. Therefore, leadership is just a natural gift. Leaders are not developed; they are discovered.

However, many authors and leaders oppose the idea that leadership is inherent. They agree that leadership is based on the qualities of a leader but believe that these qualities can be learned. They believe that ordinary people can develop leadership skills. The tremendous increase in leadership books, seminars, and courses is a testament to this perspective.

Adding to the confusion are other arguments regarding the nature of effective leadership. Is it based on the qualities or behaviors of leaders? Is leadership unrelated to the leaders themselves? Are followers more important than leaders? Are leaders just one part of the entire leadership phenomenon? Are other situational factors, like economic and political forces, more important than either the qualities or behaviors of a leader? Finally, are there any universal leadership principles? In other words, are there common elements shared by all successful leaders or does success depend on the unique circumstances that each leader faces?

## Finding Four Factors

While I was sorting through these unending disputes, I was asked to do a presentation for a seminar, which would be attended by participants in community leadership programs. I decided that I could not simply tell them that no one can agree on a definition of leadership. I also was not going to explain all of the differing theories and leave them dazed and confused. I wanted to offer them something that was both meaningful and useful.

This led me to a new approach. I knew that people disagreed. Researchers, authors, professors, leaders, and students had different views, but I began to wonder if there were common themes. Were there areas of agreement, no matter how small, among these varying approaches? Was there a solid foundation for building effective leadership? I went back to my books and began to search through what I had read.

During my search for answers, I found a certain amount of agreement regarding the basic aspects of leadership. It was not obvious at first but, after looking closely, similarities began to emerge. I began to see the same ideas, the same concepts over and over. Additionally, I saw that these aspects of leadership were never seriously questioned. Although disagreements still existed, these facets of leadership went largely unchallenged.

I initially developed the *Four Factor of Effective Leadership* to communicate these common themes. Since developing the initial presentation, I have given the seminar dozens of times to thousands of people throughout the country. As I continued to read, study, and practice leadership, I consistently found more support for the four factors. Over time, I refined my ideas and added more detail to the presentation.

The four factors are my framework for thinking about leadership. One of my students coined the term, *mental filing cabinet*, to explain this process. The four factors are not another *flavor of the month* management strategy. This is not a book that attempts to compete with other ideas about leadership. Instead, the four factors are categories designed to help you organize and integrate the vast amounts of information on leadership.

The four factors are influence, integrity, inspiration, and improvement. *Influence* is the process of controlling self and persuading others. *Integrity* involves personal credibility and trusting relationships. *Inspiration* explores the importance of purpose and shared vision and *improvement* relates to personal growth and the development of others.

The factors are not an attempt to resolve the arguments surrounding the subject of leadership. They are simply intended to provide you with a meaningful definition of leadership and a proven path for leadership development. The factors include both qualities and behaviors. They include who the leader is and what she does. The word factor is defined as something "that actively contributes to an accomplishment, result, or process." Each of the four factors actively contributes to the process of effective leadership.

The factors also provide a path for leadership development. They do this in a number of ways. First, they provide areas for assessment. Aspiring leaders can evaluate their potential in each of the four factors, and existing leaders can assess their current level of effectiveness. To assist in this process, I have provided a brief *Factor Quotient* self-assessment at the end of the chapters that deal with the four factors.

Second, the factors are presented in order of importance. This provides a clear starting point for improvement. If you are struggling with the first factor, you should focus there, before beginning to work on the other factors. Third, the factors are cumulative. They build upon each

other, with the first factor forming the foundation. Success with the later factors will be severely undermined by weaknesses in the earlier ones.

However, I want to make it clear that no one is perfect in any of these four areas. You can be more or less successful, but there is always room for improvement. Especially for new leaders, it will be important to determine when you are doing well enough in a particular factor to begin working on the next.

## Factor Fiction

Anyone who has attended school has taken multiple choice tests. The tests usually offer four or five possible answers for each question. The student's job is to choose the right one. If you know the correct answer, this is a fairly straightforward process. However, if you are unsure, then it can be very difficult. There are a number of strategies for dealing with this confusion. One of these strategies is to eliminate any incorrect answers. Sometimes it will be clear that at least one answer does not fit. By eliminating this option, the odds of success increase.

The subject of leadership is certainly more complex than a single question on a multiple choice test, especially since there are an unlimited number of options. However, the same basic strategy can be used to uncover the most effective definition of leadership. If you can eliminate some incorrect definitions, this will increase your chances for success.

Four concepts are commonly confused with leadership. They are power, personality, position, and popularity. Those who equate *power* with leadership believe that leaders have control over the actions of others. *Personality* is the notion that leadership is solely based on perception. In other words, it does not matter who you are, just who you seem to be. Some believe that leadership requires a formal *position* and the authority which that position confers. Finally, many think that leadership is the same as fame, celebrity, or *popularity*. In the following chapters, each of these *Factor Fiction* concepts will be explained in more detail and contrasted with the four factors of effective leadership.

## The Importance of Ideas

The purpose of this book is to build a useful definition of effective leadership. It is not my definition of leadership. In fact, that is the last thing that I would want you to believe. The strength of this book is that it does not

merely represent my thoughts and opinions. It is an organized collection of leadership wisdom that was discovered in the writing, research, and experiences of many different individuals. The *Factor Foundation* section at the end of each chapter shows how the four factors related to numerous influential leadership models.

Why is it so important to have a correct definition of leadership? Why does it matter what you believe? Is theory as important as taking action and getting results?

Finding a correct definition of leadership is important because your beliefs determine how you act and feel. My undergraduate and graduate education was in counseling and psychology. One of the primary tenets of cognitive psychology is that your thoughts largely determine your behavior and feelings. Inaccurate beliefs lead to ineffective actions and negative feelings. Accurate beliefs lead to effective actions and positive feelings. If these statements are true, your definition of leadership will have a tremendous impact, good or bad, on the effectiveness of your actions as a leader.

For example, imagine playing a sport without knowing which sport you were playing or what the purpose of the sport was. Should you shoot the ball, kick it, hit it with a stick, or throw it to a teammate? Is this a team sport? How do they keep score? It would be very difficult to make effective decisions on any course of action, because you would not have a clear understanding of what to do or why to do it. It is the same way with leadership. An unclear definition will lead to confusion, uncertainty, and inaction. An incorrect definition will also lead to failure. It would be like trying to play basketball in the middle of a soccer game. A good definition of leadership is essential. As a leader, you need to understand the game you are playing. This book is designed to help you develop that understanding.

### One Caution

As I present seminars in leadership and personal effectiveness, I am aware of the stereotype of the motivational speaker. Many criticize this kind of speaker for making success seem too easy. However, this is a misunderstanding of the terms *simple* and *easy*. *Simple* means straightforward and uncomplicated. The opposite of simple is complex. Complex issues are those that are confusing or hard to understand.

In contrast, the word *easy* means effortless. Difficult is the opposite of easy. Therefore, something can be simple, but not easy. Specifically, something can be simple to understand but not easy to do. For example, it is relatively *simple* to lose weight. You need to eat right and exercise more. However, it is certainly not *easy* to lose weight, but it is not difficult because you fail to understand the process. It is difficult because it takes self-discipline and restraint.

Similarly, it is fairly simple to run a marathon, just start running and do not stop until you have gone 26.2 miles. I recently completed my first marathon and, although it was not quite that simple, it certainly was not confusing. I bought some running shoes, found a training plan online, and started running. It was simple, but it was not easy. Similarly, the four factors of leadership are simple to understand but not necessarily easy to accomplish.

In this book, I hope to persuade you to believe four simple ideas.
- Everyone can be a leader.
- Leadership begins with you.
- Leadership is a relationship.
- Leadership produces positive change.

The next chapter examines the *me-first* principle and its relationship to the four factors. Each of the following chapters describes one of the four factors of effective leadership. The final chapter concludes with a new definition of leadership.

### Factor Focus
1. Who is the worst boss you ever had?
   a. What made them so ineffective?
   b. What are five qualities of ineffective leaders?
2. Who is the best boss you ever had?
   a. What made them so effective?
   b. What are five qualities of effective leaders?

# Inside-Out

Leadership is personal. It's not about the corporation, the community, or the country. It's about you. If people don't believe in the messenger, they won't believe the message. If people don't believe in you, they won't believe in what you say. And if it's about you, then it's about your beliefs, your values, and your principles.

- Jim Kouzes and Barry Posner     *Credibility*

### A Starting Point
Peter Drucker is the author of more than thirty books on leadership and management. His work has been translated into twenty languages, and he is widely considered the father of modern management. He is the founder and honorary chairman of the Leader to Leader Institute, which is dedicated to developing effective leadership in the social sector. I will use his definition of leadership as a starting point. In his introduction to *The Leader of the Future* he says simply that "the only definition of a leader is someone who has followers." This may seem simplistic, but it has tremendous implications.

It is common for people to think they are leaders despite the fact that they do not have any followers. John Maxwell, author of the New York Times Bestseller *The 21 Irrefutable Laws of Leadership,* contends that "if you think you are leading, but no one is following, you are only taking a walk." Too many people, who think they are leaders, are only out for a walk. Their leadership does not meet the basic criteria of Drucker's definition.

Followers are a necessary component of leadership, but followers are not just a necessary evil. I have met teachers who would love their jobs if not for the students and counselors who would love their work if not for the clients and all their problems. Leaders sometimes wish to lead without the intrusion of followers, but leadership requires followers. That is why Drucker's definition is so important.

Leaders who resent followers are usually drawn to leadership by the promise of power, position, and popularity. They want leadership for what it will do for them. Later in the book I will examine why that approach is ineffective. For now, it is important to note that followers make leadership possible, but they also make leadership powerful. Mary Parker Follett supports this view and believes that leadership is based on "power with others." Drucker's definition shows us that true power resides mainly in followers, not leaders.

The freely chosen actions of followers are the substance of leadership. Meaningful change requires the combined efforts of multiple individuals. If you want to change your oil, you can do it by yourself, but if you want to change the world, you need followers.

Leadership is not an individual activity. It is ultimately an interpersonal activity. Effective leaders see the potential that followers have to contribute to a meaningful cause. They understand that they need followers to achieve anything worthwhile. Because of this, they value the people they lead.

After accepting Drucker's definition, I began to wonder how leaders attract followers and why people choose to follow a particular leader. I quickly discovered that I was not the first person to ask these questions.

### Looking Inward

Jim Kouzes and Barry Posner, co-authors of *The Leadership Challenge,* conducted extensive research on the leadership qualities that people desire. They surveyed hundreds of thousands of people on the six inhabited continents. Their method was simple. They provided a list of leadership qualities and asked people to choose the qualities they most admired in leaders. The survey has been an ongoing project for more than fifteen years. In that time, there has been an amazing level of stability in the answers. Only four qualities were chosen by more than 50% of respondents. In other words, the majority of people agreed on only four of the leadership qualities. The third edition of their book shows the most recent results.

- Honest              88%
- Forward-Looking     71%
- Competent           66%
- Inspiring           65%

This list is significant for at least two reasons. First, it supports the idea that leadership begins with you. Leadership is about who you are. It is about developing the qualities that attract willing followers. Leadership development begins as personal development. This temporarily takes the focus off of the followers and puts it on the leader. If you want followers, you need to become the kind of person that people will follow. You need to intentionally develop the qualities that people desire in leaders.

Second, it is important because of the qualities that were not chosen. Competence was valued by the majority of respondents, but expertise was not. This is an important contrast. Apparently, people do not expect their leaders to be perfect or superhuman. They do not expect flawless performance. Many people are hesitant to pursue leadership opportunities because they do not see themselves as experts, but followers simply expect competence. Unfortunately, too many of them do not get it from their leaders. Similarly, intelligence was not selected by the majority of participants in the study. This is congruent with Daniel Goleman's research in *Emotional Intelligence*, which indicates that, in leadership, emotional competencies are more important than cognitive abilities.

## Learning Leadership

One of the classic questions in leadership concerns whether leaders are born or made. In other words, is leadership an inherent talent or can it be learned? Together, Drucker and Kouzes and Posner provide us with the answer to this question. Being an expert or a genius is not a prerequisite for leadership. Leadership is simply having followers, and people will follow leaders who are honest, inspiring, forward-looking, and competent. In countless seminars, participants agree that all of these qualities can be learned and practiced. You can learn to become the kind of person that people will follow. You can become an effective leader.

## Prepare for Takeoff

I was 19 years old before I had the opportunity to fly in an airplane. Now, I fly on a regular basis. One of the most painful parts of any flight is listening to the pre-flight instructions from the crew members. After talking you through the complex art of connecting your seatbelt and ominously reminding you that your seat cushion doubles as a flotation device, they proceed to discuss the procedures for handling a loss in cabin pressure.

It goes something like this, "if the plane experiences a loss of cabin pressure, oxygen masks will drop down from the ceiling. . . If you are traveling with small children, please attach your mask first and then help your child." In essence they are saying, "take care of yourself first." In this kind of emergency situation, the implications are clear. If you do not take care of yourself, you may lose your ability to care for others. The same is true in leadership. Leadership begins with you. I call this the *me-first* principle.

## Me-First

The concept of *me-first* is a clear theme in the research and writing on personal effectiveness and leadership development. In 1990, Stephen Covey published *The Seven Habits of Highly Effective People.* Since then, the book has sold more than ten million copies. Covey's seven habits begin with three habits of personal effectiveness and three habits of interpersonal effectiveness. The final habit pervades all the other habits. He argues that private victory is the foundation for public victory and that someone cannot practice habits four through six until they have mastered the first three.

In 2005, Covey wrote *The Eighth Habit: From Effectiveness to Greatness.* The eighth habit is "finding your voice and inspiring others to find theirs." Within this final habit was the same pattern as in his previous book. Greatness begins with self and moves out to others.

- Personal Effectiveness
    - o Habit 1: Be Proactive
    - o Habit 2: Begin with the End in Mind
    - o Habit 3: Put First things First
- Interpersonal Effectiveness
    - o Habit 4: Think Win-Win
    - o Habit 5: Seek First to Understand, then to be Understood
    - o Habit 6: Synergize
- Overall Effectiveness
    - o Habit 7: Sharpen the Saw
    - o Habit 8: Find Your Voice and Inspire Others to Find Theirs

In *Good to Great,* Jim Collins presents evidence that great organizations are due in part to "Level 5 leaders." He offers five progressive levels that lead to the pinnacle of leadership. According to Collins, great

leadership begins with individual performance and proceeds through increasing degrees of involvement with others.

- Level 1: Highly Capable Individual
- Level 2: Contributing Team Member
- Level 3: Competent Manager
- Level 4: Effective Leader
- Level 5 Leader: Extreme Personal Humility and Intense Will

In *The Fifth Discipline: The Art and Practice of the Learning Organization*, Peter Senge provided a framework of five leadership disciplines for developing successful organizations.

- Personal Mastery
- Shared Vision
- Team Learning
- Mental Models
- Systems Thinking

Although the book was designed to foster organizational effectiveness, Senge writes that "these might just as well be called the leadership disciplines as the learning disciplines. Those who excel in these areas will be the natural leaders of learning organizations." He notes that personal mastery is the foundation for both leadership and organizational effectiveness.

Daniel Goleman profoundly influenced the fields of psychology, education, and leadership. In *Emotional Intelligence,* he demonstrates that intellectual abilities are less important for success than was previously thought. He offers a new standard for success marked by five competencies. These competencies were refined from five to four in *Primal Leadership.* Again, the *me-first* pattern is clear.

- Self-Awareness
- Self-Regulation
- Empathy
- Relationship Skills

By promoting the principle of *me-first,* it might seem as if I am suggesting that you should not try to influence others or change the world.

That is not true. I am just emphasizing the importance of *sequence*. If you want to change the world, it is important how you proceed. Leadership begins with you, but it does not end there. It starts with you, extends to those closest to you, and then moves beyond to the broader world. The sequence is crucial. In *How Leaders Lead*, Ken Blanchard and Brian Tracy contend that "effective leadership starts on the inside and moves out." In other words, you need to put your oxygen mask on first, before you try to help others.

The following quote, from the tomb of an Anglican bishop buried in Westminster Abbey, further illustrates the importance of sequence. Notice how his goal remains the same, but his approach changes dramatically.

> When I was young and free and my imagination had no limits, I dreamed of *changing the world*. As I grew older and wiser, I discovered that the world would not change, so I shortened my sights somewhat and decided to change only *my country*. But it too seemed immovable.
>
> As I grew into my twilight years, in one last desperate attempt, I settled for changing *my family*, those closest to me, but alas, they would have none of it. And now as I lie on my deathbed, I suddenly realize:
>
> If I had only *changed myself first*, then by example I would have changed *my family*. From their inspiration and encouragement, I would then have been able to better *my country*, and, who knows, I may have even changed *the world*.

In *Deep Change: Discovering the Leader Within*, Robert Quinn, professor of organizational behavior at the University of Michigan's Graduate School of Business, suggests that leaders need to "learn the paradoxical lesson that we can change the world only by changing ourselves." He compares leaders to counselors, since the goal of both groups is to "influence and change the behavior of others."

In counseling, "effectiveness – bringing change in another person – is dependent on change in the therapist," and the same is true for leadership. "When we have successfully experienced a deep change, it inspires us to

encourage others to undergo a similar experience. . . Having experienced deep change in ourselves, we are able to bring deep change to the systems around us." However, many leaders reject the *me-first* approach.

## You-First

Picture the following scenario. A married couple with a problematic relationship attends a marriage seminar looking for relief. Each is there hoping that the other person will recognize their own flaws and the need for change. As they listen to the wisdom of experts, they are listening for words that support their negative view of the other person. They are also listening for tips on how to change the other person. The focus is external, not internal. You can imagine the scene during one of the sessions.

**John:** "Did you hear that?"

**Jane:** "Hear what?"

**John:** "She's talking to you."

**Jane:** "Who is?"

**John:** "The speaker. She just explained why you shouldn't act the way you do. You are the person that creates problems in our marriage."

**Jane:** "What are you talking about? I didn't hear that!"

**John:** "Of course you didn't. You never listen; not to me, not to the speaker, not to anyone. I don't know why we even came here. You're not even paying attention. Would you like me to take notes for you? You could learn a lot from this speaker. She's an expert."

**Jane:** "Oh, she's an expert alright, and I am listening. What I hear her saying is that you're the problem, and you need to change. This only confirms what I heard on Oprah last week."

You get the idea. Both parties are looking outside of themselves for solutions. Neither person is looking internally. The same thing happens at leadership and management conferences. Managers, supervisors and team leaders arrive with one question. "How can I get the people in my area to do

what I want them to do?" As with the marriage seminar participants, the focus is on others, instead of self. Their approach to leadership is *you-first*, instead of *me-first.*

Quinn confirms the prevalence of the *you-first* phenomenon. "When we see the need for deep change, we usually see it as something that needs to take place in someone else." In *Leading Change,* James O'Toole argues that the reason leaders fail to bring about changes in others is because they are personally unwilling to change. They expect from others something that they cannot or will not do.

Guy Kawasaki, author of *Rules for Revolutionaries,* presents ten rules for innovative leaders. Rule 9 is "never ask people to do something that you wouldn't do." Dale Carnegie, in *How to Win Friends and Influence People,* also cautions against the *you-first* approach and provides support for *me-first* leadership. "Do you know someone you'd like to change and regulate and improve? Good, I'm all in favor of it, but why not begin on yourself?"

### Control the Things you can Control
The principle of *me-first* is significant because you can only control yourself. Although you want to influence the behavior of others, and this is a requirement of leadership, you only have absolute control over yourself. The Serenity prayer asks for "the serenity to accept the things I cannot change, the courage to change the things I can, and the wisdom to know the difference." This is similar to my father's advice. When I would complain about circumstances beyond my control, he would calmly counsel me to "control the things I could control."

My dad's words echo the findings of Stephen Covey. In *The Seven Habits of Highly Effective People,* he explains that effective people spent their time and energy in their "*circle of influence,*" the people and situations in which they had some opportunity for impact. Family, friends, co-workers, and one's community are within the circle of influence.

In contrast, ineffective people spent their time and energy in the "*circle of concern.*" This realm includes all the things that affect your life, but upon which you can have little influence.

I have added a smaller circle to Covey's model. I call it the *circle of control* (see the diagram below). The circle of control includes only that over which you have absolute control, yourself. You can only completely control your choices. You cannot control events or others. This is made clear in the following quote by Viktor Frankl, a Jewish psychiatrist and survivor of the Nazi concentration camps, "the one thing you can't take away from me is the way I choose to respond to what you do to me. The last of one's freedoms is to choose one's attitude in any given circumstance."

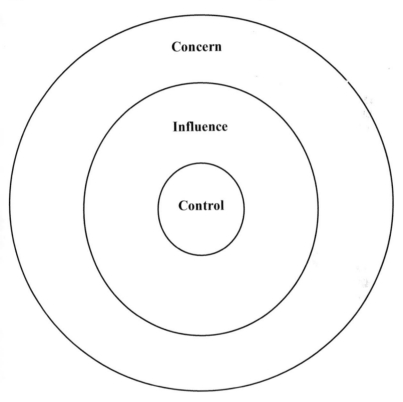

* Diagram adapted from Stephen Covey's *Seven Habits of Highly Effective People*

Similarly, the following quote from Charles Swindoll can be found in the locker rooms of athletic teams throughout America. It reinforces the importance of focusing on *me-first.*

The longer I live, the more I realize the impact of attitude on life. Attitude, to me, is more important than facts. It is more important than the past, than education, than money, than circumstances, than failures, than success, than what other people think or say or do. It is more important than appearance, giftedness or skill. It will make or break a company, a church, a home. *The remarkable thing is we have a choice everyday regarding the attitude we will embrace for that day. We cannot change our past... we cannot change the fact that people will act in a certain way. We cannot change the inevitable. The only thing we can do is play on the one string we have, and that is our attitude. . .* I am convinced that life is 10% what happens to me and 90% how I react to it. And so it is with you. [italics mine]

Athletes cannot control the weather, the referees or umpires, the crowd, field conditions or other players. They can only control themselves. That is why successful coaches, like effective leaders and fathers, encourage their players to control the things they can control.

This advice is not new. In the first century A.D., Epictetus, a Roman slave and Stoic philosopher, encouraged his followers to "make the best use of what is in your power, and take the rest as it happens." Marcus Aurelius, philosopher and Emperor of Rome, proclaimed that "your life is what your thoughts make it." In other words, if you can control your thoughts, you can control your life.

Modern psychologists support the ideas of these ancient philosophers. For example, the concept of "locus of control" was developed by Julian Rotter. People with an internal locus of control attribute their success and failure to their own actions and beliefs. In contrast, people with an external locus of control cite luck, environmental forces, biological traits, and supernatural events as the cause of their actions and life circumstances. In actual practice many people do not have a consistent locus of control. They adopt an internal locus of control when experiencing success and an external locus of control when experiencing failure. In other words, they praise themselves when they win and blame others if they lose.

Jim Collins, in *Good to Great,* refers to this in terms of "the mirror and the window." When ineffective leaders experienced success, they looked in the mirror and congratulated themselves for their efforts. When

they failed, they looked out the window to their followers and other circumstances, like the economy or unfavorable market conditions, to explain the problem. Effective leaders did the opposite. They went to the window to give the credit for success to followers and favorable circumstances, while taking a look in the mirror to examine their potential role in contributing to failure.

People's locus of control is even more crucial because of the principle of self-fulfilling prophecy, which explains that people often act in ways that cause their beliefs to come true. For example, if a leader believes that her people are lazy, she will check on them constantly and question their productivity. In doing so, she often contributes to their lack of motivation and initiative.

People with an external locus of control believe they are powerless, so they do not try to influence events. They allow events and other people to control their lives. On the other hand, people with an internal locus of control do their best to influence their lives. In doing so, they find that they are powerful and their perspective is reinforced.

Effective people tend to have an internal locus of control. Covey referred to this as being "proactive," and it is the first of the seven habits of highly effective people. In *The Success Principles,* Jack Canfield lists personal responsibility as the first and most important of more than fifty success principles. He explains that, in order to have success, you must believe that you are responsible for success. You, and no one else, are responsible for creating the life that you want. If you look to other people as the source of your success, you will be disappointed.

### Moving Out
This brings me back to the circles. Covey argues that as you work in your circle of influence it expands and you can affect events in a wider sphere. At the same time, you are decreasing the area within the circle of concern. To extend my father's advice, by controlling the things you can control, you gain an ability to influence things that were formerly beyond your reach. I believe that this process actually starts in the circle of control. You must first focus on self, which expands your influence with others, and eventually the rest of the world. The following diagram illustrates this process.

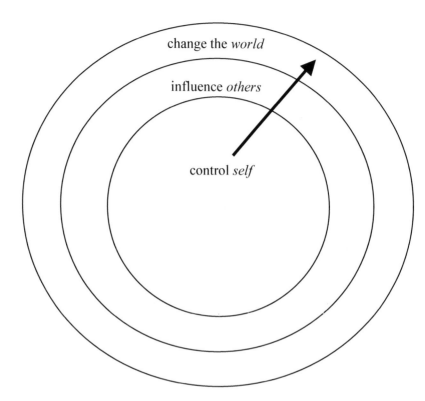

In contrast, as ineffective people focus on their circle of concern, they neglect their circle of influence. This causes their circle of concern to actually expand, thus shrinking their circle of influence. Additionally, neglecting to control yourself causes a loss of influence and an increase in overwhelming concerns. The following diagram illustrates this process.

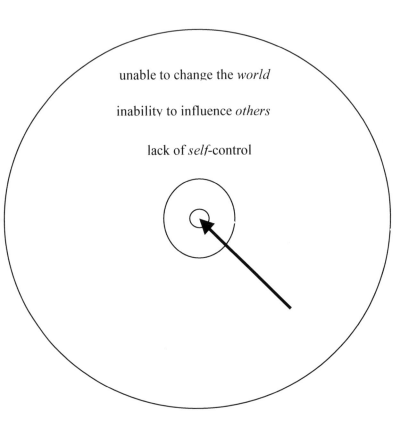

unable to change the *world*

inability to influence *others*

lack of *self*-control

Many people spend their commute and/or their work day listening to political talk show hosts articulate the problems of society and the opposing political party. These issues are largely contained within the circle of concern. Listening to these shows causes anxiety, anger, and frustration. Unfortunately, there is no real outlet for these emotions. This experience rarely leads to worthwhile action. Instead, it causes overwhelming concern about events over which you have no control and little influence. This is why some experts recommend a *news fast* to give yourself a break from the negative feelings engendered by these programs.

I recognize that there are opportunities to influence the political process on a local, state and national level and that it is important to be aware of what is happening in the world around you. However, those

opportunities are much less frequent than the daily opportunities to influence your friends, family, and associates. The point is that the time could be better spent. For example, Zig Ziglar recommends that if you want to be successful, you should enroll in "automobile university." He cites stories of people who have learned different languages, enhanced their management skills, and improved their marriages by simply listening to audio books and materials during their daily commute. I am a strong proponent of this approach.

The point is that you have choices in how you spend your time. Time spent learning how to control yourself and influence others is more valuable than time spent listening to news or talk radio, which keeps you focused on your circle of concern. Effective leaders focus on *me-first*, while ineffective leaders take a *you-first* approach.

### Internal and Interpersonal

The *me-first* principle is woven throughout the book. Each of the four factors of effective leadership has two dimensions. The first dimension is *internal*, the qualities and characteristics that need to be developed within yourself. It is what you need to do on your own.

The second dimension of each factor is *interpersonal*. It is the way you transfer personal mastery into positive relationships. It explains the process of moving from being an effective person to becoming an effective leader.

The *internal* and *interpersonal* dimensions of leadership are integrated. For example, in the first factor, I propose that leadership is *influence*. An effective leader influences, controls, and disciplines herself and then influences others. As Peter Drucker says in *The Effective Executive*, people "who do not manage themselves for effectiveness cannot expect to manage their associates and subordinates."

Similarly, the second factor, *integrity*, implies that the foundation of any relationship is trust. This is an interpersonal requirement for a leader. Covey argues that personal trustworthiness is a prerequisite for trust. Additionally, Kouzes and Posner reinforce the importance of a leader's credibility.

Additionally, the leader must have a strong personal mission. This is the basis for the third factor, *inspiration*, which requires the interpersonal ability to clearly and persuasively articulate a shared vision. Finally, in the fourth factor, *improvement*, a leader needs a commitment to personal development and lifelong learning. This commitment extends into the interpersonal realm as the leader develops others. Leadership is the integration of these *internal* and *interpersonal* dimensions. This is illustrated by the four factors model.

### The Four Factors Model

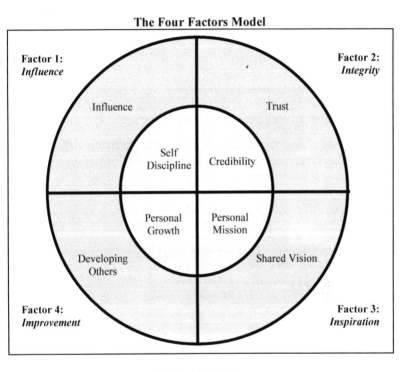

### Factor Features

In addition to the internal and interpersonal dimensions of each factor, there are a number of other common features in the following chapters.

*Factor Feat* – A brief story that illustrates the factor.

*Factor Figure* – A leader who exemplified the factor.

*Factor Failure* – An infamous leader whose life illustrates the factor fiction.

*Factor Fiction* – A leadership myth, which is contrasted with the factor.

*Factor Focus\** – Questions to help you reflect on the four factors.

*Factor Future\** – Suggestions for applying what you've learned.

*Factor Facts\** – Resources with information on each of the four factors.

*Factor Finder\** – Links to online assessments and practical tools.

*Factor Foundation\** – Support for the four factors from other authors.

*Factor Quotient* – Opportunity to rate yourself on the skills for each factor.

\* new to the revised version

## Factor Focus
1. Review the leadership qualities that people admired.
    a. What is your strongest quality?
    b. What is an example of how you demonstrated that quality?
    c. What is your weakest quality?
    d. What is an example of how you struggled with that quality?
2. How could you expand your circle of control?
3. Who are the most important people in your circle of influence?
4. How could you expand your circle of influence?
5. Who needs to be in your circle of influence?
6. What is the primary issue in your circle of concern?

## Factor Finder
*Locus of Control*
http://www.dushkin.com/connectext/psy/ch11/survey11.mhtml
- Short assessment determines if you have an internal or external locus of control.

http://www.wilderdom.com/psychology/loc/LocusOfControlWhatIs.html
- Brief overview of locus of control with links to additional resources.

## Factor Foundation

| | |
|---|---|
| **Collins**<br>*Good to Great* | Level 5 Leadership |
| **Covey**<br>*The Seven Habits of Highly Effective People* | Personal Effectiveness precedes Interpersonal Effectiveness |
| **Goleman**<br>*Emotional Intelligence*<br>*Primal Leadership* | Emotional Intelligence |
| **Kouzes & Posner**<br>*The Leadership Challenge* | Qualities People Admire in Leaders |
| **Maxwell**<br>*Developing the Leader Within You* | Leadership is Being the Kind of Person People will Follow |
| **Quinn**<br>*Deep Change* | The Leader Within |
| **Senge**<br>*The Fifth Discipline* | Five Disciplines |

# Factor 1
## *Influence*

Executives who do not manage themselves for effectiveness cannot possibly expect to manage their associates and subordinates.

- Peter Drucker    *The Effective Executive*


Leadership is influence, nothing more, nothing less.

- John Maxwell    *The 21 Irrefutable Laws of Leadership*

### Factor Feat
### *"Wild" Bill Holden*

"Wild" Bill Holden was an unemployed 56-year old Arizona resident with two bad knees and quite a few extra pounds. His knees were so bad that he needed reconstructive surgery. Unfortunately, he could not afford to pay for it, but Bill was not sitting at home feeling bad for himself. Why not? He was also a die-hard Chicago Cubs fan and when he heard that former Cubs player and Cubs announcer Ron Santo lost both legs to diabetes, he wanted to help. His goal was to raise $250,000 for diabetes research and to create greater awareness about the disease.

But how did an unknown, middle-aged, former teacher get people to donate their money? He decided to go for a walk, a very long walk, from Arizona to Chicago. The trip covered more than 2,100 miles and included some very rough terrain and extreme weather. From January to July, he put one foot in front of the other until he reached his destination.

Along the way he was included in a documentary on the life of Ron Santo and featured on ESPN. He raised both money and awareness, simply because he took a walk; a walk on knees so bad that it was hard for him to stand, much less walk. In fact, doctors told him not to try it. What was Bill's perspective? "Sure I'm sore. Sure it hurts. But how can I complain about having sore knees when Ron Santo doesn't even have any legs?"

Bill Holden wanted to influence others. He wanted to make an impact. He was concerned about the effects of juvenile diabetes. How did he make a difference? He exercised self-discipline. He endured tremendous pain and expended considerable energy. He did what he could do. In the process, he got the attention of people across the country. His simple act of self-mastery had a significant effect on the actions of people he had never met. In fact, a doctor from Indiana heard about his story and offered to reconstruct both of his knees at no cost.

Wild Bill's Walk teaches an important lesson about leadership. Before you can influence others, you have to control yourself. In *Mastering Self-Leadership,* Charles Manz and Christopher Neck contend that "if we ever hope to be effective leaders of others, we must first be effective leaders of ourselves." In fact, as Bill Holden's story demonstrates, exercising self-control is often all that is required to influence others.

## Internal Dimension
### *Self-Discipline*
My wife and I have two young daughters. In order to teach good manners to our children, we do not say many of the words we formerly used in daily conversation. We have little difficulty avoiding major profanity, vulgarity, and obscenity. However, my wife has also outlawed more common words that are not universally considered offensive. Terms like stupid and shut-up are just two that have been banned. My wife has restricted my use of these words because she does not want our children to say them. She understands the principle of *me-first.* We cannot expect our children to behave differently than they see us behaving. If we want our children to act in a certain way, we need to act that way. This takes considerable self-discipline. Our self-control or lack thereof will be reflected in the behavior of our daughters. Our influence over them is constrained by our influence over ourselves.

Self-discipline is the theme of Sal Severe's book, *How to Behave so Your Children will Too.* After working for years as a psychologist, he discovered that many children's behavioral problems were directly related to the inappropriate actions of their parents. In contrast with most parenting manuals, his book was directed at parents and their behaviors. It was not designed as a guide for regulating children's behavior. "Parents need to understand that their children's behavior is often a reflection of their own

behavior. That's what makes this book unique. It does not focus on what children do wrong. It teaches parents what they can do differently."

The same principle applies to leadership. This was made clear by Peter Drucker in *The Effective Executive.*

> Management books usually deal with managing other people. The subject of this book is managing oneself for effectiveness. That one can truly manage other people is by no means adequately proven. But one can always manage oneself. Indeed, executives who do not manage themselves for effectiveness cannot possibly expect to manage their associates and subordinates. Management is largely by example. Executives who do not know how to make themselves effective in their own job and work set the wrong example.

Drucker's contention is supported by the research of Kouzes and Posner. One of their five exemplary practices of leadership is "model the way." Leaders have to be willing to exhibit the behaviors that they desire to see in others. This was the message of Gandhi when he said, "If you would change the world, you must be the way you want the world to be."

John Maxwell, in *The 21 Irrefutable Laws of Leadership,* calls this the "Law of Magnetism." He argues that you get what you are. If you do not like the quality of your followers, consider the quality of your leadership. If you want to attract better followers, you need to become a better person. For example, if, on a scale of 1 to 10, you are an 8, then you will attract people who are 6s and 7s. If you want to attract people who are 8s and 9s, you must become a 10. His point is that the people around you are a reflection of you. If you do not like the reflection, you need to change the person in the mirror.

Peter Senge proposes self-mastery as the first of five leadership disciplines. Similarly, Jim Collins says that being a "highly capable individual" is the first of five levels of leadership. In *Leaders,* Warren Bennis and Burt Nanus offer four strategies employed by effective leaders. The third strategy is "deployment of self," which involves positive self-regard and knowing and utilizing one's strengths.

Self-control has long been recognized as the foundation of success. Writing in the sixth century B.C., Lao Tzu, the father of Taoism and author of the *Tao Te Ching,* declared that "mastering others is strength. Mastering yourself is true power." In other words, it might actually be more difficult to exercise self-discipline than interpersonal influence. The primacy of self-discipline is confirmed by Plato. Around 400 B.C., the Greek philosopher proclaimed that "the first and best victory is to conquer self."

If you fail to successfully influence others, you should look first at yourself as the potential cause. Thomas a Kempis, a German monk and author living in the 15th Century, cautioned "be not angry that you cannot make others as you wish them to be, since you cannot make yourself as you wish to be." In other words, frustration with, and focus on, the behavior of others is often misplaced.

Furthermore, people often expect more from others, than they are willing to do themselves. This is the exact opposite of effective leadership. Henry Ward Beecher was a well-known abolitionist preacher and advocate of women's suffrage in America during the mid 18th century. He encouraged a greater focus on self-mastery than mastering others. "Hold yourself responsible for a higher standard than anybody else expects of you. Never excuse yourself. Never pity yourself. Be a hard master to yourself-and be lenient to everybody else."

Dee Hock, founder of Visa International, quantifies the importance of self-leadership and offers specific areas of focus. "If you seek to lead, invest at least 50% of your time leading yourself—your own purpose, ethics, principles, motivation, conduct." How many people spend as much time trying to lead themselves as they do trying to lead others?

If you want to be an effective leader, then you must develop self-discipline. This involves understanding and controlling your thoughts, actions, and feelings, increasing self-awareness, and developing an ability to delay gratification.

### H3 – Head, Heart & Hands
How does a person gain control over her behavior? How can someone develop self-discipline? Psychologists believe that actions are primarily based on thoughts and beliefs. People do what they think will work. Whether something *works* is usually measured by whether an action

leads to positive feelings. In other words, people do what they think will make them feel good. This is a basic principle of motivation. To control your behavior, it is necessary to know what you believe and what makes you feel good. You also need to be clear about the results that your current actions are producing.

In an effort to clarify this process, I have developed a model that called *H3* (head, heart, hands). The *head* represents your thoughts, the *heart* your emotions, and the *hands* your actions. Any effort to control your life must begin with your head, by examining your thoughts and beliefs.

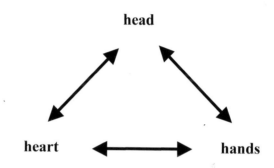

For example, stereotypes are incorrect generalizations about a particular group of people. Stereotypical beliefs (*head*) lead to discriminatory actions (*hands*). Any effort to change discriminatory actions must start with the stereotypical beliefs. Similarly, stereotypical beliefs (*head*) about a group of people lead to feelings of prejudice (*heart*), which are manifested by discomfort, anxiety, or fear when encountering representatives of that group. People's actions (*hands*) in turn are motivated by the desire to avoid these negative feelings (*heart*).

This process explains why beliefs about leadership are so important. Your beliefs (*head*) have a tremendous impact on your actions (*hands*). Just as stereotypical beliefs (*head*) lead to discriminatory behavior (*hands*) and prejudicial feelings (*heart*), inaccurate or incomplete beliefs (*head*) about leadership will lead to ineffective leadership actions (*hands*), which cause feelings of frustration with self and anger toward others (*heart*).

## *Mirror, Mirror on the Wall*

The first step to gaining control over yourself is to become aware of the content and effect of your existing beliefs. However, most people are not actively conscious of many of their beliefs. This is why Daniel Goleman argues that self-awareness is a prerequisite for self-regulation. You cannot control yourself until you understand yourself.

The ancient Greeks believed that self-awareness was essential. The maxim "Know Thyself" was considered so important that it was inscribed on the Oracle at Delphi. Self-knowledge includes understanding strengths, weaknesses, interests, values, purpose, personality, and styles of communication, conflict resolution, problem-solving, and leadership. Many of the assessments in the factor finder section at the end of the chapter will help you to improve your self-awareness.

If you would like to recommend other self-assessments, please send an email to me at dave@drendall.com  I may add your submission to the four factors resources on my website www.drendall.com and to future editions of the book.

## *Managing Marshmallows*

Daniel Goleman uses the following story to demonstrate the importance of self-regulation. In the early 1960s psychologist Walter Mischel initiated a study that would continue for the next thirty years. The research began with an experiment. A four-year old was brought to a small lightly furnished room with a table in the center. A researcher in a white coat entered and set a marshmallow on the table. The child was given these instructions. "First, the marshmallow is yours. You can eat it if you want. Second, I'll leave the room for fifteen to twenty minutes. Third, when I return, if the marshmallow is still on the table, I'll give you a second marshmallow."

Some children ate the marshmallow even before hearing all of the instructions, they were so eager to taste the candy. Others listened intently but ate the marshmallow shortly after the researcher left. Some tried in vain to resist the temptation, but gave in before the time elapsed. A number of children managed to refrain from eating the marshmallow for the full fifteen minutes. Their strategies varied. They sat on their hands, closed their eyes, sang songs, and walked around the room. They did anything they could to

distract themselves from their desire to eat the marshmallow and, as promised, they were rewarded with a second marshmallow.

These two groups of children were then followed into adulthood. Those that demonstrated self-discipline during the marshmallow challenge had a higher level of social competence, which included personal effectiveness, assertiveness, and frustration tolerance. They also earned higher SAT scores by an average of 210 points.

The point of this story is that the ability to delay gratification is linked with effectiveness. It is the hallmark of self-discipline. Self-discipline is not, as some believe, caused by a lack of interest in pleasure or enjoyment. It is the ability to endure pain in the short-term, in order to experience greater pleasure in the long-term. As John Maxwell says, "you can play now and pay later, or pay now and play later, but you always have to pay. If you play first, you end up paying a lot more later."

Retirement savings offers a clear illustration of this concept. If you play now, you spend your money as you earn it and enjoy the benefits immediately. However, once you retire, if you can even afford to, you will have to pay, by living with less. In contrast, if you pay now, you invest your money for the future and cannot make use of it immediately. However, when you reach retirement age, you will be able to enjoy life without worrying about your financial needs. Effective people and effective leaders pay now so that they can play later.

Robin Sharma, author of *The Monk Who Sold His Ferrari,* wrote that "it is impossible to create a great life without self-discipline and dedication." Dedication implies commitment and perseverance. Leadership is difficult and requires courage and stamina. Leaders without self-discipline do not have the capacity to sustain their efforts when encountering hardship. Those who can delay gratification, endure momentary difficulties in order to achieve greater success in the future.

John Maxwell, in his book *Developing the Leader Within You,* explains that "self-discipline is the price tag of leadership." Stephen Covey's research indicates that effective people exercised self-discipline by acting on their priorities. He calls this putting "first things first." Again, the connection between self-awareness and self-control is evident. You have to know what are priorities are, before you can act on them.

Self-leadership is difficult. In a *Fast Company* article, Alan Deutschman cites research that 90% of heart bypass patients failed to change their lifestyle to avoid future health problems. Sometimes the change was as simple as taking a pill each day. Even a crisis that threatened their life was not enough to ignite their self-discipline. When I ask people in my seminars and classes why they have failed to achieve goals, the most common response is a lack of self-discipline.

At its roots, leadership is not about getting other people to do what you want them to do. It is about getting yourself to do what you want yourself to do. Again, this is simple but not easy. Effective leaders control their thoughts, feelings, and behaviors. Their actions align with their most important priorities. They have developed self-awareness and the ability to delay gratification. They know that the ability to influence others is the *second marshmallow*, the reward for exercising self-discipline. Understanding and influencing yourself provides the foundation for understanding and influencing others.

## Interpersonal Dimension
### *Influence*
Influence with others is the most basic element of leadership. Leaders affect the thoughts, feelings, and actions of others. Joseph Rost, in *Leadership in the 21st Century,* defines leadership as "a relationship based on influence." Similarly, John Maxwell writes that "influence is the definition of leadership." The first influence strategy is to understand people. Understanding others is a prerequisite for influence. As Stephen Covey said, "In order to have influence, you must first be influenced." Effective leaders have a deep understanding of, and appreciation for, their followers.

### *Empathy*
Empathy is the experience of truly understanding another person. It is seeing things from the other person's perspective. This is similar to Covey's first habit of interpersonal effectiveness, "seek first to understand, then to be understood." Additionally, Daniel Goleman cites it as one of the four competencies of emotional intelligence. Similarly, Daniel Pink, in *A Whole New Mind,* argues that empathy is one of six essential aptitudes that will be essential for success as society moves from the information age into the conceptual age.

Why is this so important? Why begin a discussion of influence with the concept of empathy? Because, as Covey argues, "Next to physical survival, the greatest need of a human being is . . . to be affirmed, to be appreciated, to be understood."

Empathy involves four basic steps. The first step is listening. This is more difficult than it sounds. People do not usually listen. Instead, they are busy thinking about something else or their response. Step two is understanding. This means taking what you have heard and trying to make sense of it, to see things from the other person's perspective. The third step is to communicate what you have understood to the other person. This gives them the opportunity to confirm your understanding, which is the final step.

If you did not understand the other person accurately, she can provide further clarification. When this occurs, you must go back to step one, which is listening, and go through the process again. This can be time-consuming and difficult, but it is worth the effort. According to Henry Ford, "if there is any one secret of success, it lies in the ability to get the other person's point of view and see things from that angle, as well as from your own."

### *Levels of Listening*
Covey proposes five different levels of listening, with empathy at the highest level.

- *Ignoring:* Failing to listen
- *Pretend listening:* Trying to give the impression of paying attention.
- *Selective listening:* Only hearing what you want to hear.
- *Attentive listening:* Listening carefully and with interest.
- *Empathic listening:* Seeing things from the other person's perspective.

Empathic listening sets an important precedent in your relationship with followers. When you listen to others, they will usually listen to you. As Covey says, "Because the other person's need to be understood has been satisfied, we are much more likely to . . . be understood ourselves." When you take time to understand others, it also shows that you care, which is an important aspect of Factor 2, *Integrity.* Additionally, it helps you to develop a shared vision that inspires others, a crucial step in Factor 3, *Inspiration.* Furthermore, empathy is a powerful method for learning and personal growth, which is the focus of Factor 4, *Improvement.*

### *Effective Listening*

Below are a number of practical suggestions to help you listen effectively. This is often called active listening.

- *Reflect*: Repeat back what the other person has said to you.
- *Summarize*: Attempt to briefly paraphrase the key points the other person has shared.
- *Clarify*: Ask for additional information and a more detailed explanation.
- *Focus on feelings*: Look for the emotions that they are experiencing.
- *Ask open-ended questions:* Ask questions that require more than just one word responses.
- *Use "I" statements:* Take responsibility for your responses by starting sentences with "I."
- *Be aware of body language:* Don't cross arms, frown, or otherwise communicate disinterest.
- *Maintain eye contact:* Don't stare, but demonstrate your interest with consistent eye contact.

- *Don't judge:* Don't tell the other person why they are wrong.
- *Don't ask why:* Asking why usually makes people feel defensive.
- *Don't offer advice:* Solutions aren't valued until you have truly understood the problem.

### *Universal Needs*

It is important to understand each person as an individual. However, there are some fairly universal human traits and desires. Abraham Maslow developed a hierarchy of human needs. He believed that every person's desires could be organized into five categories.

- Level 1: *Survival* – needs of basic existence (food, clothing and shelter)
- Level 2: *Security* – a sense of safety
- Level 3: *Belonging* – relationships and community
- Level 4: *Self-esteem* - confidence and a feeling of importance
- Level 5: *Self-actualization* - desiring a significant and meaningful life

Lower level needs, such as survival and security must be met before people will be motivated to fulfill higher level needs, such as self-actualization. For example, someone who is starving is more motivated by survival than the desire for relationships.

Awareness of these general needs allows you to understand particular influence strategies. For example, Dale Carnegie did an exhaustive study of human relations, which is detailed in *How to Win Friends and Influence People.* He explained that people do not like to be criticized. Criticism usually leads to justifications, defensiveness, and rejection. He cites the work of Freud and Maslow, who demonstrate that all people have a longing to be important. Criticism minimizes people's importance and is rarely accepted.

On the other hand, sincere appreciation fulfills people's desire for significance. That is why *The One Minute Manager,* by Ken Blanchard and Spencer Johnson, encourages leaders to "catch people doing things right." However, it is important to note the emphasis on sincerity when expressing appreciation. Insincere praise is flattery and is not an effective strategy for influencing others.

### *Tune in to WII-FM*

In college, I took a course in industrial & organizational psychology. During that class, I watched a woefully outdated video about persuasion. It included a man with the demeanor and appearance of a used car salesman giving a very animated explanation of the influence process. Despite the obvious problems with the presentation, I still remember one key point. He said that when you want to influence someone you have to tune in to the radio station, WII-FM (What's In It For Me). In every interaction, you need to be aware that this is the question in the forefront of people's minds. You need to give a clear and compelling answer if you want to influence them. Too often, you are busy telling people what's in it for you. This is ineffective. As Dale Carnegie said, most people are concerned about their own needs and any attempt to influence them must focus on "the benefit that accrues to them." Effective leaders influence people by understanding and meeting their needs.

Not only is empathy an important quality for leaders, it is precisely the quality lacking in those who have been diagnosed as psychopathic. Psychologist Alfred Adler declared that "it is the individual who is not interested in his fellow men who has the greatest difficulties in life and provides the greatest injury to others. It is from among such individuals that all human failures spring." These individuals would put their oxygen mask on first but would not proceed to help the person next to them. In fact, if

their oxygen mask was not working properly, they would probably take one away from their neighbor.

This reinforces an important caveat to the *me-first* principle. It does not mean *me first, last, and everywhere in between.* Leadership begins with you, but it does not end there. Leadership is having followers. Those who are unable to move beyond their own needs and interests will ultimately fail in life and in leadership.

### *Motivation*

Cognitive psychologists believe that behavior is not motivated by past events as much as beliefs about the potential consequences of actions. People tend to act in ways that are calculated to bring pleasure, while avoiding actions that could lead to pain. In other words, people's actions are focused on the future, specifically beliefs about the connection between current acts and future consequences. If you want others to change their behavior, you have to influence their thoughts. Specifically, you need to show them how the desired behavior change will lead to positive feelings. These positive feelings result from fulfilled needs. This is simply the process of *H3*, applied to others instead of self.

Expectancy theory proposes that people will be motivated to act if three conditions are met. First, they believe they have the ability to successfully perform the desired act. Second, they will be rewarded for that act. Third, the reward will be something that they value. This is important because not everyone has the same abilities. Similarly, people value different things. For example, people may be at different levels of Maslow's need hierarchy. Leaders must understand both the abilities and the values of those they lead in order to exercise influence.

Expectancy is specifically focused on the *head* in the *H3* model. Expectancies are beliefs about one's abilities, the potential for success, and the likelihood of meaningful rewards. Therefore, leaders exert influence by affecting these beliefs. This can be done in four ways. First, recognize and praise people for their skills. Second, present an optimistic outlook regarding the probability of success. Third, clearly explain the positive consequences of success. Fourth, ensure that rewards are meaningful by tailoring them to the needs of each individual. People feel good (*heart*) when they believe (*head*) that their actions (*hands*) will lead to valuable rewards.

40

## Factor Figure
### *Mahatma Gandhi*

Many great leaders demonstrated the relationship between self-discipline and influence. However, the life of Mahatma Gandhi stands above the rest. Biographer B. R. Nanda wrote that Gandhi's "life was . . . one long struggle for self-mastery." He endured frequent imprisonment and nearly died during the course of at least one hunger strike. He lived a simple life of "poverty and austerity," just like the majority of the Indian people. For example, Gandhi sometimes walked as far as 40 miles in a single day. This was in stark contrast to the lifestyles of the country's political elite. As a leader and teacher he believed that his life was an "eternal object lesson."

His philosophy of passive resistance required him to undergo significant pain and humiliation without seeking revenge. He consistently influenced others by enduring "self-suffering." As a living example of nonviolent protest, he had a tremendous influence on Martin Luther King Jr. and the civil rights movement in America. The effectiveness of his approach was also demonstrated by the peaceful overthrow of communism in many eastern European countries. Ultimately, he sacrificed his life for the cause of Indian independence. He was assassinated shortly after India became a free nation.

## Factor Failure
### *Jim Jones*

In 1978, more than 900 men, women, and small children committed mass suicide or were murdered in Jonestown, Guyana. Their deaths followed the murder of a United States congressman who had recently arrived to investigate the group known as the Peoples Temple. There were reports that Jim Jones, after whom the town was named, was holding people against their will. Jones and members of his group left the United States for Guyana, a small country in northeastern South America, to establish a utopian community and escape the scrutiny of government and law enforcement officials. Apparently, Jones saw himself as a messiah and claimed, at various times, to be God, Buddha, and Lenin.

Although many joined the group willingly, Jones eventually used force and the threat of violence to keep members from deserting. In fact, one news report alleged that a member was killed after announcing his desire to leave the group. Furthermore, there was evidence that the mass suicide was not completely voluntary. Although many people willingly

drank a tainted beverage, others appeared to have been injected with poison against their will and others were shot. Parents and other adults were also responsible for poisoning more than 300 children in the group. In resorting to coercion, Jones failed to meet Drucker's first test for leaders. He had captives, not followers.

Some of Jones' erratic behavior can be attributed to his lack of self-discipline. It was alleged that he physically and sexually abused members of his cult, and he was once arrested for soliciting a male prostitute in California. Additionally, he could not control his addiction to drugs. Because of this, he lost the trust of some of his closest advisors. Jones' actions demonstrated his incredible desire for control. The gruesome deaths at Jonestown provide a painful illustration of the importance of self-discipline and the inadequacy of power and coercion.

## Factor Fiction
### *Power*

Power is often confused with leadership. Some think of power as the ability to make people do what they want them to do. Many want to be leaders because they think it will give them control over the actions of other people. However, command, dominance, force, and coercion are not elements of effective leadership.

Warren Bennis and Burt Nanus write that "leaders lead by pulling rather than pushing . . . by inspiring rather than ordering . . . by creating achievable, though challenging, expectations and rewarding progress toward them, rather than by manipulating . . . by enabling people to use their own initiative and experiences rather than by denying or constraining their experiences and actions." Founder and CEO Emeritus of Visa International, Dee Hock, argues that "control is not leadership . . . If you don't understand that you work for your mislabeled 'subordinates,' then you know nothing of leadership. You know only tyranny."

Many relate the exercise of power to military leadership. However, in 1942, Norman Copeland wrote in *Psychology and the Soldier* that "leadership is the art of dealing with human nature. . . It is the art of influencing a body of people through persuasion or example to follow a line of action. It must never be confused with drivership – to coin a word - which is the art of compelling a body of people by intimidation or force to follow a line of action."

Peter Drucker, the father of modern management, doubted that power over others was even possible. "That one can truly manage other people is by no means adequately proven." His skepticism was supported by the lives and deaths of martyrs, people that refuse to denounce their beliefs, even when threatened with death. Similarly, former prisoners of war and concentration camp survivors demonstrate the limitations of coercion and force.

Victor Frankl, a Jewish psychiatrist and author of *Man's Search for Meaning*, who survived imprisonment in a Nazi concentration camp, argued that people were free to choose their response to cruel and brutal treatment. He believed that inhumane behavior did not justify an inhumane response. His life was a testimony to the truth of his claims. If the threat of death is not enough to gain control over another person, this is not a likely avenue for effective leadership. Furthermore, it is obvious that most leaders do not have the option of threatening their followers with death.

French and Raven conducted considerable research on the subject of power. They described five main types of power:

- *Referent:* Followers' relationship with and respect for the leader.
- *Reward:* The ability to offer meaningful rewards to followers.
- *Legitimate:* Organizational or political position and authority.
- *Expert:* Knowledge, experience and skills.
- *Coercive:* Threats and punishment.

Of these five types of power, coercive power is the least effective and causes the most conflict between leaders and followers. People seem to naturally resist any attempt to control their thoughts, feelings, or behavior.

Leadership is not power over others; it is influence with others. Max DePree, former CEO of Herman Miller and author of *Leading without Power*, asserts that leadership must be freely given by those who follow. If this is true, how does a leader influence others? What are the prerequisites for influencing others? The final three factors will answer these questions and extend your understanding of the influence process.

Factor 2 is *Integrity*, which includes credibility and trustworthiness. Your ability to influence others is based on their assessment of your credibility. Factor 3 is *Inspiration*. In the words of

43

Bennis and Nanus, "influence works by attracting and energizing people to an exciting vision of the future." Factor 4 is *Improvement*. Leaders influence others by helping them to expand their abilities and reach their potential.

## Factor Focus

1. "Wild Bill" Holden influenced others by controlling himself. Can you think of a time where your example influenced another person, either positively or negatively?

2. Who was the most influential person in your life? What made them so influential?

3. What specific actions could you take to lead yourself? How much time do you currently spend on these activities?

4. One way to master the H3 concept is to practice with your biggest pet peeve.
   a. What do you think, feel & do when it happens?
   b. What could you think that would change your feelings and actions?

5. Why is an understanding of self so important for leaders?

6. What are some ways that you could "pay now," so that you can "play later?" How can you use this concept with those you lead?

7. Why do we often fail to listen empathically?

8. Which level of listening do you practice most often? How could you move to the next level?

9. If people are tuned in to WII-FM, how can you find out what they want and need?

10. What needs are you trying to fulfill through your work?

11. How can you reward the people that follow you and those that lead you? Which of these rewards would be the most effective? Why?

12. Think of a time when someone tried to "drive" you using coercion.
    a. How did you respond?
    b. How did you feel?

13. Why do so many people try to rely on power? Why is the use of power so problematic?

14. Dee Hock argues that leaders work for their followers, not the other way around.
    a. Do you think this is true? Why or why not?
    b. If it is true, how can a leader work for their followers?

15. What is your greatest personal success?
    a. How did you achieve it? Why did you do it?

b.   What lessons can you learn from this experience that will guide you as you help others to succeed?
16.  What is your greatest leadership moment? How did you influence people?

## Factor Future

1.   Begin keeping a journal in which you reflect on your experiences.
2.   Read a biography of Gandhi and/or watch the movie.
3.   Read selected books from the factor facts section.
4.   Complete self-assessments in the factor finder section.
5.   Work through self-assessments with your team. Discuss the results and implications for working together.
6.   Practice listening empathically to someone in your circle of influence. What was it like to try to listen empathically? How did the other person respond?

## Factor Facts

Bennis & Goldsmith     *Learning to Lead*
- Great exercises and self-assessments for new and developing leaders

Buckingham & Clifton     *Now, Discover Your Strengths*
- Helps you to focus on your strengths and the strengths of those you lead (includes free StrengthsFinder assessment)

Burns     *Feeling Good: The New Mood Therapy*
- Learn how to control your thoughts, feelings and actions

Carnegie     *How to Win Friends and Influence People*
- A classic. Good examples of, and timeless principles for, influencing self and others.

Cialdini     *Influence*
- Another classic. Learn the six primary methods for influencing others.

Gladwell     *Blink*
- Learn the value of cultivating and listening to your intuition.

Gladwell     *The Tipping Point*
- Learn how influence works in the context of large groups and society.

Nanda     ‹     *Mahatma Gandhi: A Biography*

Sony Pictures     *Gandhi (190 minutes, DVD release 2001)*

### *Factor Finder*

Self assessments are a great way to enhance your self-awareness. Below is a list of various online surveys related to leadership and personal effectiveness.

*Emotional Intelligence*
http://glennrowe.net/BaronCohen/EmpathyQuotient/EmpathyQuotient.aspx
60 question EQ test. Gives your score and how it compares to others.

*Stress Management*
http://www.franklincovey.com/fc/library_and_resources/stress_assessment
Measures your level of stress and your habits of personal renewal.
Offers an explanation of your results and suggestions for improving your responses to stress.

*Seven Habits of Highly Effective People*
http://www.franklincovey.com/fc/library_and_resources/self_scoring_7_ha bits_personal_feedback
Determine your effectiveness in living each of the seven habits.
Printable survey form with scoring instructions.

*Leadership Style*
http://www.nwlink.com/~donclark/leader/survstyl.html
Requires user to print and manually score the assessment.
Results indicate if you have a participative, delegative or authoritative style.
Doesn't provide in-depth explanation of these styles.

http://www.pao.gov.ab.ca/toolkit/tools/whats-your-leadership-style.htm
Requires user to print and manually score the assessment.
Results indicate if you have a task/initiating structure style or a relationship/consideration style and provides brief explanation of the styles.

*Time Management*
http://cub.wsu.edu/lead/library/resources/Time%20Management/The%20Ur gency%20Index.pdf
Results indicate your dependence on urgency to complete tasks.

*StrengthsFinder*
https://www.strengthsfinder.com/
Discover your top five strength themes
(free with purchase of the book, *Now, Discover Your Strengths*)

*REAL Leadership*
http://estore.injoy.com/real/real.asp
Based on John Maxwell's "REAL" Leadership
(Relationships, Equipping, Attitude, Leadership)
Good explanation of the REAL model and your results

*Personality*
http://www.humanmetrics.com/cgi-win/JTypes2.asp
Results indicate your personality type based on Jung's typology
- introvert vs. extrovert
- intuitive vs. sensing
- thinking vs. feeling
- perceiving vs. judging

Relates your scores to famous people with similar typology
Offers in-depth explanations of your score/type

*Temperament – Keirsey-Bates*
http://www.advisorteam.com/temperament_sorter/register.asp?partid
Requires free registration, Provides good explanation of your temperament

*Various*
http://www.mhhe.com/business/management/buildyourmanagementskills/menu.html
Select "self-assessments"
- Active Listening Skills
- Emotional Intelligence
- Do you have what it takes to be a leader?
- Preferred Organizational Structure
- Valuing Diversity
- Decision-Making
- Flexibility
- Leader-Member

Great information on the particular assessment.
Clear results, most with detailed explanations.

Which Star Wars character are you?
http://www.seabreezecomputers.com/starwars/

Which Star Trek Character are you?
http://www.seabreezecomputers.com/startrek/

*Leadership Practices Inventory*
http://www.lpionline.com/lpi/
Based on Kouzes and Posner's Leadership Challenge
(requires survey administration and purchase of license)
- *Model the Way*

*21 Irrefutable Laws of Leadership*
http://www.injoy.com/OnlineTools/assessment.aspx
Based on John Maxwell's book with the same title
21 different assessments for each leadership law
Requires free, brief online registration (email address, name, zipcode)
- *Magnetism: Who you are is who you attract*
- *Buy-In: People buy into the leader, then the vision*
- *Sacrifice: The leader must give up to go up*
- *Influence: The true meaning of leadership is influence*

*17 Indisputable Laws of Teamwork*
http://www.injoy.com/OnlineTools/assessment.aspx
Based on John Maxwell's book with the same title
17 different assessments for each teamwork law
Requires free, brief online registration (email address, name, zipcode)
- *Chain: The strength of a team is impacted by its weakest link*
- *Catalyst: Winning teams have player who make things happen*
- *Bad Apple: Rotten attitudes ruin a team*

### Factor Foundation

| | |
|---|---|
| **Bass**<br>*Leadership and Performance Beyond Expectation*<br><br>**Burns**<br>*Leadership* | Transformational Leadership<br>- Idealized Influence |
| **Bennis & Nanus**<br>*Leaders* | Four Strategies<br>- Deployment of Self |
| **Covey**<br>*The Seven Habits of Highly Effective People* | Seven Habits<br>- Habit 1: Be Proactive |

| | |
|---|---|
| **Collins**<br>*Good to Great* | <u>Level 5 Leadership</u><br>- Level 1: Highly Capable Individual |
| **Finzel**<br>*The Top Ten Mistakes Leaders Make* | <u>Top Ten Mistakes</u><br>- Dictatorship in Decision-Making<br>- The Top-Down Attitude |
| **Goleman**<br>*Emotional Intelligence*<br>*Primal Leadership* | <u>Four Competencies</u><br>- Self-Awareness<br>- Self-Regulation |
| **Kouzes & Posner**<br>*The Leadership Challenge* | <u>Five Exemplary Practices</u><br>- Model the Way |
| **Maxwell**<br>*The 21 Irrefutable Laws of Leadership* | <u>21 Irrefutable Laws</u><br>- Magnetism: Who you are is who you attract<br>- Buy-In: People buy into the leader, then the vision<br>- Sacrifice: The leader must give up to go up<br>- Influence: The true meaning of leadership is influence |
| *The 21 Indispensable Qualities of a Leader* | <u>21 Indispensable Qualities</u><br>- Self-Discipline: The first person you lead is you<br>- Positive Attitude: If you believe you can, you can<br>- Initiative: You won't leave home without it<br>- Responsibility: If you won't carry the ball, you can't lead the team |
| **Morris**<br>*True Success*<br>*The Art of Achievement* | Self-Awareness |
| **Senge**<br>*The Fifth Discipline* | <u>Five Disciplines</u><br>- Personal Mastery |

# Factor Quotient
## *Influence*

Please read each of the statements listed below.
Record your level of agreement with each statement in the blank to the left.
Total your answers and refer to the scoring key at the end of the assessment.

*5 Strongly Agree    4 Agree    3 Not Sure    2 Disagree    1 Strongly Disagree*

---

|        |     |                                                          |
|--------|-----|----------------------------------------------------------|
| _____  | 1.  | I consistently *delay gratification.*                    |
| _____  | 2.  | I have developed strong *self-awareness.*                |
| _____  | 3.  | I control my *thoughts, feelings, and behaviors.*        |
| _____  | 4.  | I am aware of how my behavior influences others.         |
| _____  | 5.  | I understand my *needs* and motivations.                 |
| _____  | 6.  | I demonstrate *empathy* when interacting with others.    |
| _____  | 7.  | I understand the needs and *motivations* of others.      |
| _____  | 8.  | I praise others for their abilities.                     |
| _____  | 9.  | I recognize the limitations of *power* and control.      |
| _____  | 10. | I tailor rewards to the needs of each individual.        |

_____  **Total Score**

**Scoring Key**

**41-50**   Great, maximize your abilities in this factor
**31-40**   Good, continue to fine-tune certain aspects of this factor
**21-30**   You may want to focus attention on this factor
**< 26**   This factor might be a barrier to your leadership effectiveness

# Factor 2
## *Integrity*

If people anywhere are to willingly follow someone - whether it be into battle or into the boardroom, the front office or the front lines - they first want to assure themselves that the person is worthy of their trust.

- Jim Kouzes and Barry Posner                    *The Leadership Challenge*


Trust is the emotional glue that binds followers and leaders together. The accumulation of trust is a measure of the legitimacy of leadership. It cannot be mandated or purchased; it must be earned.

- Warren Bennis and Burt Nanus                    *Leaders*


### Factor Feat
#### *Tylenol*
In 1982, seven people died after unknowingly taking Tylenol laced with cyanide. As a result of this tragedy, Johnson & Johnson, the makers of Tylenol, faced a dilemma. Their company specialized in medical products. Their purpose was to help people lead healthy lives. The widely publicized Johnson & Johnson credo started with the following phrase. "We believe our first responsibility is to the doctors, nurses and patients, to mothers and fathers and all others who use our products and services. In meeting their needs everything we do must be of high quality." Now, this responsibility was being tested.

How did they respond? In one of the most notable examples of public integrity, Johnson & Johnson recalled more than 30 million bottles of Tylenol and took immediate steps to thwart further tampering by developing elaborate new packaging. Their actions were consistent with the noble ideals of their credo.

Many doubted if Tylenol could ever recover from this disaster. In fact, in other similar problems at other companies, concerns about loss of reputation often cause company leaders to delay responses or deny responsibility. However, Johnson & Johnson's response actually bolstered people's confidence in the company. This is not unusual. When companies make mistakes and resolve them, customers actually become more loyal than they would be to companies with whom they have not had a negative experience. It may be that adversity provides an opportunity to see the true character of a company or individual.

Tom Morris, in *True Success,* describes the origins of the word integrity, which means wholeness and harmony. Consider the term structural integrity. It means that a building literally holds together, that it is sound, that it can be trusted and relied upon and that you are safe within its walls. People want to know that their leaders have integrity, to know that it is safe to follow.

Morris goes on to describe Plato's three part formula for influence and persuasion, which included logos (logical argument), pathos (emotional appeal) and ethos (character and integrity). Without integrity, influence falters. It is indispensable. "Ethical action produces a form of strength grounded in trust that nothing else can duplicate." This is reinforced by Donald Phillips in *Lincoln on Leadership.* "The architecture of leadership, all the theories and guidelines, falls apart without honesty and integrity." As with the other factors, integrity begins inside the leader.

## Internal Dimension
### *Credibility*
Stephen Covey argues that personal trustworthiness is a prerequisite for trust. Kouzes and Posner refer to this quality as credibility. Leaders must be honest, reliable, consistent, and authentic. They must demonstrate personal integrity in their words and actions. Integrity requires significant self-discipline and is the foundation of effective leadership. There are four basic components to credibility; they are character, competence, caring, and confidence.

### *Character*
Tom Morris declares that character is one of the seven timeless requirements for success. Character implies honesty. Remember that

honesty was chosen as the most important quality of a leader in the study by Kouzes and Posner. Effective leaders tell the truth.

A classic definition is that "character is who you are when no one is looking." It is a representation of your true self. Frances Hesselbein, former CEO of the Girl Scouts and Chairperson of the Board of the Leader to Leader Institute, argues that "leadership is who you are, not what you do. Character determines results."

Character refers to harmony between your words and your actions, between your private and public self. Psychologists refer to this as authenticity, congruence, or genuineness. This principle is so common that it is found in many clichés like "practice what you preach" and "walk your talk." When I was a child, I heard a traveling preacher put it this way. "Your walk will talk and your talk will talk, but your walk will always talk louder than your talk will talk." A more succinct version is that "actions speak louder than words."

Max DePree illustrates this aspect of character in his book *Leadership Jazz*. His granddaughter, Zoe, was born prematurely, and the baby's father was not there to care for her. Max stepped in to help both his daughter and her child. The baby was so small that Max could slide his wedding ring up and down her arm.

On one visit to the hospital, a nurse gave him specific instructions. He should stay with the baby and gently rub his fingers over her body. As he did this, he should talk to her. The nurse said that it was important for the baby to connect his voice and his touch. DePree proposes that this is a powerful lesson for leadership. Leaders must match their voice and their touch. There must be congruence between what they say and what they do.

In his textbook *Management,* professor Ricky Griffin explained that the best way to have an ethical company is for leaders to model ethical actions. People emulate the actions of leaders. Punishments and sanctions do not work if the leaders' behavior is not consistent with their words or the stated policies of the company. Quinn refers to this as the "hypocrisy gap." Effective leaders are constantly devoted to closing the gap between their actions and words.

"To be good is noble; but to advise others on how to be good is nobler and no trouble." This cynical quote from Mark Twain illustrates the dilemma of character. It is necessary, but very difficult. People often fail to live up to even their own stated ideals. Character is another example of the difference between simplicity and difficulty. It is certainly simple to understand the concept, but it can be very difficult to practice. Furthermore, character is not the only requirement for credibility. Leaders must also be competent, caring, and confident.

### Competence

In my seminars, I ask people if they have ever had an incompetent manager. Very few people raise their hands, they just laugh out loud. Most people think I am asking a rhetorical question. Unfortunately, it seems that incompetent leaders are a universal phenomenon. The tremendous popularity of the Dilbert cartoon series is based on the seemingly ubiquitous incompetence of managers.

Like honesty, competence is one of the four qualities that people admire in leaders. Both Covey and Drucker cite competence as an essential element of credibility. To illustrate the relationship between character and competence, consider the following example. My four year old daughter may be honest, but I do not trust her to drive my car to the mall. I do not trust her because she does not know how to drive. She lacks competence. John Maxwell, in his book *The 17 Qualities of a Team Player,* calls this "countability." People need to be able to count on their leaders. Competence involves a certain level of consistency and reliability.

There are two basic kinds of competence, interpersonal and technical. The need for interpersonal competence increases as a manager climbs the organizational hierarchy. At the same time, the need for technical competence decreases. Both are necessary, but leadership requires higher degrees of interpersonal competence. One of the hallmarks of interpersonal effectiveness is a genuine concern for others. Effective leaders care about their followers.

### Caring

People do not care how much you know till they know how much you care. This statement is a reminder that leadership is a human endeavor. It requires an intimate connection between leader and followers. Before

people will follow, they want to know that the leader is concerned for them and their interests.

Leadership is not a selfish pursuit. Leadership begins with you, but it does not end there. Followers make leadership possible, and they make leadership powerful. Effective leaders recognize the significance of their followers. DePree refers to this as a state of indebtedness. Leaders need their followers, as much as, or more than, the followers need their leader. A leader who does not acknowledge the reciprocity of this relationship will fail to foster the trust that is necessary for effective leadership.

### Confidence

Tom Morris contends that successful people have a strong confidence that they can achieve their goals. Another way to think of confidence is self-trust. The person who most closely observes your character, competence, and caring is yourself. Others might consider you credible, even when you are not. You must first trust yourself before you can expect others to trust you.

Many people have let themselves down so many times that they have given up. I have students who no longer set goals because they have failed to achieve them in the past. Often people question their ability to create the life they desire. They have seen their mistakes and begin to doubt their *character*. Their actions do not demonstrate that they truly *care* for their bodies, minds, hearts, and souls. Some people tell themselves lies and refuse to honestly evaluate their strengths and weaknesses. They do not have confidence because they doubt their own credibility. You must earn the right to trust yourself before you can gain the trust of others.

## Interpersonal Dimension
### Trust

Have you ever told the truth, but the other person did not believe you? Have you ever had someone doubt your *competence*, despite the fact that you had the necessary ability? Have you ever *cared* for someone, only to find that they thought you disliked them? Most people have experienced situations in which their internal characteristics were not evident to those around them. Credibility is absolutely essential for trusting relationships, but it is not enough. You must clearly and consistently demonstrate your trustworthiness, in order to gain the trust of others.

Regarding trust, Bennis and Nanus proclaim that it "is the emotional glue that binds followers and leaders together. The accumulation of trust is a measure of the legitimacy of leadership. It cannot be mandated or purchased; it must be earned." If this is true, then how can trust be earned? Since trust cannot be forced, how can you make it more likely that people will trust you?

There are five basic paths to trust. They all revolve around cultivating and communicating your credibility. You need to take what is inside of you and make it visible to others. First, you need to make and keep promises. Second, you should be open and transparent in your activities. Third, you must develop and express a genuine concern for others. Fourth, you need to continually increase your competence. Finally, you need to be willing to trust others.

### *Take it to the Bank*
Many different authors talk about trust in terms of banking. When you demonstrate credibility, you make deposits into your *trust account* with the other person. When you are dishonest, you make a withdrawal from that same account. If you make more withdrawals than deposits, you overdraw your trust account. You need a positive balance in the trust account to have effective relationships.

One of the ways to make deposits is to offer sincere praise. In contrast, criticism is a withdrawal. It seems as though people are not very good bank tellers. They tend to keep good records of criticism, withdrawals, but lose track of compliments, deposits. People can charge high bank fees for untimely withdrawals. Because of this, it is important to make at least six deposits for every withdrawal.

Another way to make deposits in your trust account is to make and keep your promises. People trust those who keep their word and do what they say they will do. In Max DePree's terms, you make deposits when your voice matches our touch. Broken promises are withdrawals, and, as with criticism, there are high fees associated with them. If you want to develop trust with a person, simply make clear promises and then deliver on those promises. Below is a list of trust account deposits and withdrawals, adapted from Covey.

| Deposits | Withdrawals |
|---|---|
| Kindness | Unkindness |
| Keeping promises | Breaking promises |
| Clear expectations | Unclear expectations |
| Loyalty to the absent | Disloyalty, duplicity |
| Apologies | Pride, Arrogance |
| Praise | Criticism |
| Transparency | Secrecy |

### *Swimming in the Fish Bowl*

Transparency is a second method for developing trust. People tend to assume the worst about others and the best about themselves. One representation of this tendency is what social psychologists call fundamental attribution error. Social psychologist, David Myers, explains that people attribute the negative behavior of others to their personality and character. People hold others responsible for their wrong actions. However, people attribute their own negative behavior to situational factors like bad luck and stressful circumstances. In other words, their personal actions are justifiable, given the situation. This is similar to the concept of locus of control discussed earlier.

Because of this tendency, it is important to be transparent. You need to provide others with adequate information about your activities so that they can make proper evaluations of your behavior. If you are secretive, people will develop ominous explanations of even the most innocuous decisions.

When I was a manager, I was involved in many activities that took me out of the office. I was on the board of directors for the local chamber of commerce, presented leadership seminars, made sales and fund raising presentations, and met with local associates. I knew that this could lead my staff to question my commitment to the company and wonder if I was working as hard as they were. If they did not see me come in to the office until ten o'clock, it would be reasonable for them to assume that I had slept late or was running errands. They had no way to know that I was actually up early for a breakfast meeting, unless I shared that information with them.

Unfortunately, many leaders feel that, if followers have an incorrect interpretation, they have no responsibility to justify themselves. Being *in charge* means not having to explain yourself to others. I took a

different approach. Each week, I printed out my schedule and posted it on my door. This allowed everyone, including people who were not in my department, to know where I was at all times. I also sent email messages giving a detailed explanation if I was going to be out of the office for an extended period of time.

The point is that trust must be actively nurtured. Transparency is one way to foster trust. This can be accomplished in many different ways. Sharing your rationale for making certain decisions, involving people in planning, communicating clearly and consistently, and relating appropriate personal information are just a few strategies.

### Love 'em and Lead 'em

The third strategy for developing trust is to demonstrate a genuine concern for others. Literally, you need to show love. "Love 'em and lead 'em" is one of Jim Kouzes' favorite phrases. It is the key theme of the book *Encouraging the Heart,* which he co-authored with Barry Posner. As with the other factors, this cannot be faked. It is not enough to pretend to care for others. It must be sincere. Dale Carnegie stressed the importance of sincerity in *How to Win Friends and Influence People.* "The principles taught in this book will work only when they come from the heart. I'm not advocating a bag of tricks. I'm talking about a new way of life."

One way to demonstrate caring is to treat other people as you would like to be treated. This simple principle provides guidance in a broad range of situations. For example, Covey emphasized the importance of "being loyal to those that are not present." When you criticize people behind their backs, your listeners conclude that you will do the same to them when they are not around.

You demonstrate caring when you help others to achieve their goals and meet their needs. Follow Dale Carnegie's advice by helping others feel important. Show them how their actions contribute to a larger cause. Ask questions about their family, their vacations, their hopes, and their fears. Spend time listening. Truly listen by practicing the four steps of empathy from chapter three. Remember their birthdays and anniversaries. Write them notes of thanks. You get the idea. It is not enough to care, you must also actively demonstrate your concern.

### *Vulnerability*

Credibility is absolutely essential for trusting relationships. Demonstrating character, competence and caring is vital, but it is not enough. You must trust others if you want them to trust you. In *Five Temptations of a CEO,* Patrick Lencioni cautions against the tendency for leaders to choose "invulnerability over trust." To trust another person is to risk disappointment, pain and loss. Many leaders find it safer and easier to stay closed-off and separate from their followers. This is counterproductive. In his extensive study of influence, Robert Cialdini discovered the principle of reciprocity. Simply put, people tend to treat others in the same manner that they are treated. If you do not trust others, they will not trust you.

### Factor Figure
#### *Abraham Lincoln*

Abraham Lincoln was the 16th President of the United States. He presided over one of the most difficult eras in American history. His administration nearly witnessed the end of the union between northern and southern states. However, he emerged from the death and destruction of the Civil War as one of the most revered figures in America.

One reason for his incredible success was a strong commitment to honesty and integrity. Indeed, historian Donald T. Phillips writes that "Without question honesty is one of the major qualities that made him a great leader." He demonstrated this honesty long before becoming President. Early in his career he was the co-owner of a general store in Illinois. His partner was an alcoholic and amassed a significant debt for the business. When the partner died, Lincoln accepted responsibility for the full amount. After a number of years, he finally repaid the debt.

Lincoln was criticized and questioned by many leaders of his time. However, even his enemies acknowledged his integrity. Phillips explains that "Lincoln's reputation for honesty and integrity, even though challenged over the years, has remained unblemished." He required integrity from those around him. As President, Lincoln fired one of his cabinet members for engaging in questionable practices. He refused to associate with people who could not be trusted. His harsh reactions to any form of dishonesty were effective because, in the words of Phillips, "Lincoln also practiced what he preached."

Lincoln was loyal to those that were not present. He did not openly criticize those with whom he disagreed. In fact, he avoided criticizing some incompetent generals even when speaking or writing to them directly. He was slow to believe negative reports about others and cautioned his advisors "never add the weight of your character to a charge against a person without *knowing* it to be true."

"Honest Abe" demonstrated astonishing competence. In situations that would have overwhelmed many leaders, he made crucial and ultimately successful decisions regarding both military strategy and political issues. His character and competence were rewarded as the American people elected him to a second term and the Union was preserved. Unfortunately, as with Gandhi; he was assassinated before he could witness the enduring success of his leadership.

## Factor Failure
### *Hitler*

The life and death of Adolph Hitler provide a disturbing illustration of the dangers of dishonesty and incompetence. His initial political success was based on deception and violence, which demonstrated his lack of character. He is widely despised for his masterful use of manipulation. Throughout his life he showed a complete lack of concern for others and an obsessive focus on himself. He used fear, hate, prejudice, and propaganda to rally the German people for war and the extermination of millions of Jews. However, his methods were not sustainable.

He lacked the competence to coordinate such an incredible military campaign. Instead of transparency, he relied on secrecy, which ultimately led to suspicion and paranoia. He was unable to trust others and they, in turn, did not trust him. Stephen Ambrose, in his book *Citizen Soldiers,* put it poignantly. "The German command structure was a disaster. Hitler's mistrust of his generals and the general's mistrust of Hitler were worth a king's ransom to the Allies." This mistrust was clearly demonstrated when German generals devised a plot to assassinate their leader. Unlike Lincoln, Hitler's goals were never fulfilled and his life ended in disgrace.

## Factor Fiction
### *Personality*

Trust requires integrity. Integrity requires credibility, and credibility requires self-discipline. Unfortunately, it is difficult and

sometimes painful to live with integrity. Because of this, many people look for a shortcut. Personality is their solution.

Personality implies that perception is more important than substance. In other words, who you are, your character, is less important than who you seem to be, your image. If people want an honest leader, then pretend to be honest. In the words of Groucho Marx, "The secret to life is honesty and fair play. If you can fake that you've got it made." It is not necessary to do the hard work of developing credibility, simply give people the impression that you can be trusted. Projecting the appropriate image is the hallmark of personality.

Personality is a rejection of the *me-first* principle. It seeks to influence others without controlling self. Covey's research demonstrates that this is a very prevalent approach in modern leadership books. Books on success and effectiveness formerly focused on character. Authors assumed that people needed to cultivate their internal life in order to be successful. However, there was a gradual move away from this approach. Character was replaced by a focus on personality and the science of impression management and image. The emphasis was on the surface instead of substance.

Many authors and leaders reject the importance of credibility through character, competence, and caring. Deception and manipulation are frequently offered as effective leadership practices. One of the often cited texts on leadership is Machiavelli's *The Prince*. Written in 1513, it offers wisdom for aspiring princes of the 16th century. The following excerpt demonstrates Machiavelli's disregard for honesty and integrity. "It is necessary for a prince wishing to hold his own to know how to do wrong, and to make use of it or not according to necessity."

For those who do not have time to read the original manuscript, there are many modern books that apply Machiavelli's ideas to leadership. Some of the titles are instructive. For example, Stanley Bing wrote a book entitled, *What Would Machiavelli Do? The Ends Justify the Meanness*. This is a classic representation of the idea that credibility is not always effective, and that, in leadership, dishonesty is a necessary evil.

In case you doubt the popularity of Machiavelli's ideas or his continuing influence, just consider the title of the recent book by Michael

Ledeen, *Machiavelli on Modern Leadership: Why Machiavelli's Iron Rules are as Timely and Important Today as Five Centuries Ago*. This is not an aberration. Below is a list of other books that glorify the value of violence, greed, and deception as tools of leadership. Titles related to the Sopranos refer to a popular HBO television series about a fictional mafia family.

-   *The New Machiavelli: The Art of Politics in Business*
    by Alistair McAlpine

-   *The Modern Machiavelli: The Seven Principles of Power in Business*
    by Ian Demack

-   *The Boss: Machiavelli on Managerial Leadership*
    by Richard Hill.

-   *The Mafia Manager: A Guide to the Corporate Machiavelli*
    by V

-   *Tony Soprano on Management: Leadership Lessons Inspired by America's Favorite Mobster*
    by Anthony Schneider

-   *Leadership Sopranos Style: How to Become a More Effective Boss*
    by Deborrah Himsel

Substituting personality for leadership is problematic for two reasons. First, it is impossible to keep up the façade of personality. People inevitably discover what you have been hiding and, when they do, the false trust that formerly existed breaks down. In the short-term, the personality approach can seem tremendously successful. However, it cannot be sustained and eventually reverses any momentary successes.

Second, pretense and deception have an influence on you. Psychologists have shown that people who consistently lie to others begin to believe those lies. It seems that something about you longs for congruence. In order to avoid the pain of lying, you start to convince yourself that you are telling the truth. The unfortunate result is that you lose touch with reality and no longer know what is true.

The perils of personality are illustrated in two classic works of literature. Oscar Wilde's *The Picture of Dorian Gray* tells the story of a man whose portrait reflected his true inner self. As Dorian Gray became increasingly involved in corruption and murder, the painting of himself as a young man became more and more disfigured. Although he attempted to hide his actions, the painting told the real story. Eventually, he attempted to destroy the painting and, in doing so, killed himself. The implication is that despite your best efforts your true character will always reveal itself.

Robert Louis Stevenson's classic tale of *Dr. Jekyll and Mr. Hyde* has a similar theme. In the story, Dr. Jekyll was a successful respected physician. He discovered a potion that allowed him to transform into Edward Hyde, a representation of the evil side of the doctor's nature. Mr. Hyde indulged in indecent acts and then returned to become Dr. Jekyll. On two separate occasions, Hyde even committed murder.

Jekyll continued to move back and forth between these two lives, unable to resist his primal desires, which were fulfilled while acting as Hyde. However, he could not maintain control of himself and the consequences of his dual life. He soon found that the potion was no longer required. He automatically transformed into Hyde each morning. His secret would not remain hidden. What he once controlled now controlled him. Finally, in a desperate attempt to escape from the evil that he became, Dr. Jekyll killed himself.

Machiavellian and mafia leadership are often defended using a philosophy that the ends justify the means. In other words, deceit is not wrong when employed for positive or pragmatic purposes. However, as is evident in the stories of Dorian Gray and Dr. Jekyll, dishonesty and violence ultimately have their own negative impact on the perpetrator.

Furthermore, despite this misplaced reverence for dishonest leaders, it is clear, from the research of Kouzes and Posner and others, that people want to follow someone they can trust. People want to be confident that their leader it telling them the truth. Trust is the foundation of any successful relationship.

To illustrate this, just think about the effects of infidelity. Once a partner has been unfaithful, the foundation of trust has been destroyed. Everything about the couple's past becomes suspect. The offended partner

does not know what to believe anymore. It is not so much the act of infidelity as the subsequent loss of trust that destroys the relationship.

I remember when I was a child, and I told a lie to my parents. After discovering my dishonesty, they told me that it would be difficult for them believe my words in the future. My lying cast doubt on my future claims.

Similarly, most people are familiar with the story of the boy who cried wolf. A young shepherd was bored with his duties and decided to get the attention of the local residents. He loudly announced that a wolf was menacing the sheep, despite the fact that no wolf was nearby. Many people rushed to his aid, only to find that he was lying. He did the same thing again with a similar result. When a wolf actually attacked his sheep, the townspeople would no longer respond to his cries.

In addition to illustrating the pitfalls of dishonesty, this story shows how leaders can often be deceived by deception. In the short-term, the shepherd boy's lies did indeed influence those around him, even after he had been caught the first time. The seeming effectiveness of dishonesty is what ensnares so many leaders.

Effective leaders reject the temptations of personality and dishonesty. They develop strong credibility by demonstrating character, competence, and caring. They trust themselves and others. Through transparency and consistently keeping promises, they earn the trust of their followers. Leadership is a relationship. It is built on a foundation of integrity and trust. The next factor, inspiration, will provide focus and direction for that relationship.

### Factor Focus

1. What was a personal or professional situation that challenged your integrity? How did you respond?
2. Why is it sometimes so difficult for us to "do the right thing?"
3. What could you do to become more worthy of people's trust?
4. What are some ways that you could match your voice and your touch?
5. What can you do to improve your competence?
6. Do you need to focus on your interpersonal or technical competence?
7. How could you cultivate a sincere concern for those you lead?

8. What have you done to undermine your confidence?
9. What could you do to increase your confidence?
10. What are three of your most important relationships?
    a. What is your current trust account balance with each of those people?
    b. What could you do to make a deposit?
11. Do you trust people until they demonstrate that they can't be trusted or do you withhold trust until they earn it?
12. Why do we often choose invulnerability instead of trust? How can we overcome this?
13. Why is it so tempting to rely on personality instead of cultivating character?
14. Can you think of an example when a leader relied on personality? What were the consequences?

## Factor Future
1. Read a biography of Lincoln and/or watch the A&E Biography.
2. Read selected books from the factor facts section.
3. Complete the self-assessments in the factor finder section.
4. Work through self-assessments with your team. Discuss the results and implications for working together.
5. Make a list of the anniversaries and birthdays of those who are close to you. Write them a short note or give a card on these important days.
6. Write a note of thanks to someone who has helped you recently.
7. Apologize to someone that you have hurt or mistreated in some way.
8. Admit to someone that you were wrong.
9. Improve your emotional bank account balance with someone who is important to you.

## Factor Facts
Ambrose                    *Citizen Soldiers*
- Provides a good review of Hitler's ineffectiveness as a leader.

Kouzes & Posner            *Encouraging the Heart*
- Clear manual for encouraging others in the workplace.

Kouzes & Posner         *Credibility: How leaders gain it and lose it, why*
                        *people demand it*
- The title says it all.

Lencioni                *The Five Temptations of a CEO*
- A short leadership fable that illustrates the five temptations leaders face.

Phillips                *Lincoln on Leadership*
- Learn leadership, and the importance of integrity, from the life of one of
the country's greatest leaders.

Stevenson               *Dr. Jekyll and Mr. Hyde*
- Excellent illustration of the pitfalls of duplicity and deceit.

Wilde                   *The Picture of Dorian Gray*
- A vivid reminder of what happens when we fail to cultivate personal
integrity.

### Factor Finder

http://www.mhhe.com/business/management/buildyourmanagementskills/menu.html
Select "self-assessments"
- *Ethical Decision-Making*
- *Active Listening Skills*
- *Conflict Style*

*Leadership Practices Inventory*
http://www.lpionline.com/lpi/
Based on Kouzes and Posner's Leadership Challenge (requires survey
administration and purchase of license)
- *Encourage the Heart*

*21 Irrefutable Laws of Leadership*
http://www.injoy.com/OnlineTools/assessment.aspx
Based on John Maxwell's book with the same title
21 different assessments for each leadership law
Requires free, brief online registration (email address, name, zipcode)
- *Solid Ground: Trust is the foundation of leadership*

*17 Indisputable Laws of Teamwork*
http://www.injoy.com/OnlineTools/assessment.aspx
Based on John Maxwell's book with the same title
17 different assessments for each teamwork law
Requires free, brief online registration (email address, name, zipcode)
*- Countability: Teammates must be able to count on each other when it counts*

---

If you know about other interesting resources, self-assessments, or application ideas, please send an email to me at dave@drendall.com I'd love to add your submission to the four factors resources on my website www.drendall.com and/or to future editions of the book.

---

### *Factor Foundation*

| | |
|---|---|
| **Bass** <br> *Leadership and Performance Beyond Expectation* <br><br> **Burns** <br> *Leadership* | <u>Transformational Leadership</u> <br> - Individualized Consideration <br> - Moral Character & Ethical Values <br> . |
| **Bennis & Nanus** <br> *Leaders* | <u>Four Strategies</u> <br> - Trust through Positioning |
| **Covey** <br> *The Seven Habits of Highly Effective People* | <u>Seven Habits</u> <br> - Habit 5: Seek first to Understand, then to be understood |
| **Finzel** <br> *The Top Ten Mistakes Leaders Make* | <u>Top Ten Mistakes</u> <br> - Putting Paperwork before Peoplework <br> - The Absence of Affirmation |
| **Goleman** <br> *Emotional Intelligence* <br> *Primal Leadership* | <u>Four Competencies</u> <br> - Empathy <br> - Relationship Skills |
| | |

| Kouzes & Posner | Five Exemplary Practices |
|---|---|
| *The Leadership Challenge* *Encouraging the Heart* *Credibility* | - Encourage the Heart Credibility |
| **Maxwell** *The 21 Irrefutable Laws of Leadership* | 21 Irrefutable Laws - Solid Ground: Trust is the foundation of leadership |
| *The 21 Indispensable Qualities of a Leader* | 21 Indispensable Qualities - Character: Be a piece of the rock - Competence: If you build it, they will come - Security: Competence never compensates for insecurity - Listening: To connect with their hearts, use your ears - Relationships: If you get along, they'll go along |
| **Morris** *True Success* *The Art of Achievement* | Seven Cs of Success - Consistency - Character |

# Factor Quotient
## *Integrity*

Please read each of the statements listed below.
Record your level of agreement with each statement in the blank to the left.
Total your answers and refer to the scoring key at the end of the assessment.

*5 Strongly Agree    4 Agree    3 Not Sure    2 Disagree    1 Strongly Disagree*

| | | |
|---|---|---|
| _____ | 1. | I have a strong character. |
| _____ | 2. | I demonstrate competence. |
| _____ | 3. | I genuinely care about those around me. |
| _____ | 4. | I have self-confidence, and I trust myself. |
| _____ | 5. | I am honest. |
| _____ | 6. | I keep my promises. |
| _____ | 7. | I conduct my affairs in a transparent manner. |
| _____ | 8. | I match my voice and touch. |
| _____ | 9. | I recognize the limitations of *personality* and image. |
| _____ | 10. | I have trusting relationships with others. |

_____ **Total Score**

**Scoring Key**
**41-50**    Great, maximize your abilities in this factor
**31-40**    Good, continue to fine-tune certain aspects of this factor
**21-30**    You may want to focus attention on this factor
**< 26**    This factor might be a barrier to your leadership effectiveness

# Factor 3
## *Inspiration*

The very essence of leadership is [that] you have a vision. It's got to be a vision you articulate clearly and forcefully on every occasion. You can't blow an uncertain trumpet.

- Theodore Hesburgh


Influence works by attracting and energizing people to an exciting vision of the future.

- Warren Bennis & Burt Nanus


Leadership is the capacity to translate vision into reality.

- Warren Bennis


### Factor Feats
#### *Melissa, Tommy & Markita*

In 1989, when she was only nine years old, Melissa Poe was inspired by an episode of the television series *Highway to Heaven,* which dealt with the negative effects of pollution. After watching the show, she was convinced that she needed to do something. She sent a letter to President George H. W. Bush requesting his assistance. While waiting for a response, she persuaded a local company to put her message on a billboard. Eventually, it appeared on 250 billboards throughout the country. Her effort generated interest from other concerned children. In response, she started Kids For a Cleaner Environment (Kids FACE).

Despite eventually receiving a disappointing response from President Bush, she wrote to Sam Walton requesting that Wal-Mart become a corporate sponsor. That letter was successful. Melissa's story was featured

in Kouzes and Posner's book, *The Leadership* Challenge and Kids FACE is now the largest youth-led environmental organization in the world, with 300,000 members throughout the United States and over 20 foreign countries.

Tommy Tighe was six years old when he was inspired by the cause of peace. He got a $500 loan from speaker and author Mark Victor Hansen's Children's Free Enterprise Bank and printed 1000 bumper stickers that said "Peace, Please! Do it for us kids." One of his first customers was former President Ronald Reagan, who lived nearby. He also sent a bumper sticker to Mikhail Gorbachev with a bill for $1.50. Gorbachev paid the bill and included a personal note in his response. Due to his accomplishment, Tommy had the opportunity to promote the cause of peace on national television, and his story appeared in the bestselling book *Chicken Soup for the Soul*. He believed that his mission was successful. Within the first two years of his peace project, he saw the fall of the Berlin Wall.

Markita Andrews' father abandoned her and her mother when she was only eight years old. Her mother worked full-time as a waitress to make ends meet, but they had a dream. After Markita graduated from college, they would take a trip together around the world. Their opportunity came sooner than that. The Girl Scouts were offering a free trip around the world to the girl who sold the most Girl Scout cookies. Despite being very shy, Markita decided to win the contest. She won the trip after selling more than 3,500 boxes of cookies and her success continued long after the trip was over. She co-authored a book, *How to Sell More Cookies, Condos, Cadillacs, Computers ... And Everything Else*, and appeared in a Disney movie that recounted her story. She continues to receive regular requests to speak at sales conventions. Like Tommy Tighe, her story inspired millions of people when it was featured in the book *Chicken Soup for the Soul* by Jack Canfield and Mark Victor Hansen.

Melissa, Tommy, and Markita illustrate a number of important lessons. Their stories reinforce each of the main themes in this book. These children demonstrated the *me-first* principle. They exhibited Factor 1, *Influence*, by first managing themselves and then influencing others. They modeled the way. They showed Factor 2, *Integrity*. People trusted them because they were genuinely committed to a cause. Their actions matched their words. They were authentic.

Their lives also illustrate Factor 3, *Inspiration*, which is the subject of this chapter. Leadership begins with a personal mission, a passion for a cause or a goal. As you take action in pursuit of your mission, you often inspire others to join you. Leadership does not start with others. It starts within you, in your heart and soul, in your deepest longings and desires. Each of these children inspired themselves before ever approaching anyone else. Their personal commitment was magnetic.

## Internal Dimension
### *Personal Mission*

The research of Kouzes and Posner shows that people admire leaders who are forward-looking and inspiring. Markita, Tommy, and Melissa exhibited these qualities. They had a mission for their lives, and they inspired others to share that vision. These two qualities seem to be closely related. People are inspired by those who are forward-looking.

The importance of looking ahead is supported by Stephen Covey. His second habit of highly effective people is "begin with the end in mind." Before you can act, you need to know what you are trying to accomplish. His third habit is "first things first," which involves taking action on your highest goals and priorities.

According to Tom Morris, the first condition of success is "a clear conception of what we want, a vivid vision, a goal or set of goals powerfully imagined." In fact, four of his seven conditions for success are related to mission. He argues that people need an "emotional commitment" to the goal and "focused concentration" on the method for achieving their purpose. People also need a "stubborn consistency" as they encounter difficulties along the way. In other words, effective leaders need purpose, passion, a plan, and perseverance.

### *Purpose*

Tommy, Melissa, and Markita each had a clear purpose. Unfortunately, most people, although they may have work-related goals, do not have a strong sense of mission. This is significant. Victor Frankl argued that purpose is the fundamental motivating factor in people's lives. Without purpose, life lacks meaning. This leads to hopelessness and despair. According to Helen Keller, "the most pathetic person in the world is someone who has sight but has no vision."

Andy Stanley, in his book *Visioneering,* says that "everyone ends up somewhere in life, some people end up there on purpose." Whether or not you are consciously aware of your purpose, you are headed in a certain direction. Your life is on a path, the question is whether it is taking you where you want to go. Mark Sanborn, professional speaker and author of *The Fred Factor,* argues that everybody makes a difference. Your actions inevitably affect the lives of others. You should not be asking "will I make a difference?" Instead, you should be asking, "what kind of difference will I make?" In his unique style, Yogi Berra confirmed the importance of purpose. "You've got to be very careful if you don't know where you're going, because you might not get there."

The importance of intentional purpose is illustrated in Lewis Carroll's classic story *Alice's Adventures in Wonderland.* Alice is a young girl who has fallen into an imaginary world and has a series of surreal experiences. At one point Alice is speaking to the Cheshire Cat.

Would you tell me please, which way I ought to go from here?

Well that depends a great deal on where you want to get to, said the cat.

I don't much care where, said Alice.

Well then, it doesn't matter which way you go, said the cat.

So long as I get somewhere, Alice added as an explanation.

Oh you're sure to do that, said the cat, if you only walk long enough.

A lack of purpose makes it impossible to choose a course of action. Aimlessness creates hopelessness. Actress Lily Tomlin is famous for saying that "I always wanted to be somebody. Now I realize that I should have been more specific." Ambiguous goals cause confusion, lead to uncertain actions, and ultimately bring about undesirable results.

To illustrate this, consider a sport that involves a target. In archery, the goal is to hit the bulls-eye, the center of the target. It is possible to measure success related to that standard. Successful athletes hit close to the

bulls-eye; unsuccessful ones do not. Similarly, successful people paint a clear picture of the target and the bulls-eye for their lives. They aim their efforts in that direction and compare their results to this pre-existing standard.

In contrast, unsuccessful people do not define the target. They proceed through life aimlessly. They have no standard with which to compare their progress. Unfortunately, as Stanley said, "everyone ends up somewhere," regardless of whether or not they had a plan. In response, these people simply define where they have ended up as the bulls-eye. They draw the target after the shot. They define the standards of success after the performance. They justify their actions by dishonestly declaring that this is where they want to be.

In contrast, effective leaders have a clear and detailed purpose that guides their decisions. They define the standard for success before beginning. Their mission provides focus and direction to their actions.

So what can you do to discover your mission? There are a number of exercises designed to help you formulate a mission. First, imagine your 80th birthday. What will it be like? Who do you want to be there? Choose three to five people who will say something about your life and consider what you would want them to say. There is also an alternate version in which you consider your funeral and ask the same questions.

Another exercise involves answering the following question. What would you do if you did not have to make money? If you were financially independent, how would you spend your time? This question is designed to uncover your true interests and preferences without the constraints of financial pressures.

Jim Collins, in his book *Good to Great,* offers a model for organizing this information. He tells a story about the hedgehog and the fox. The fox is the predator and the hedgehog, the prey. Foxes are known for being clever, and the fox is always trying new methods of capturing the hedgehog. He tries open intimidation, but the hedgehog just rolls up into a ball. The hedgehog's body is covered with sharp spikes which the fox cannot penetrate.

The fox tries to hide and catch the hedgehog by surprise. When he leaps from the bushes, the hedgehog simply rolls up into a ball. The fox uses his speed to chase down the hedgehog from behind, but the hedgehog again rolls into a ball. The point is that the fox is always trying something different. He is always devising new strategies, most of which are ineffective. The hedgehog has one clear and effective strategy, which he consistently employs.

Collins uses this story as an illustration of purpose. He argues that each person needs her own "Hedgehog Concept." She needs to discover the one thing that will provide direction to her efforts. She needs a single point of focus. This single point is found at the intersection of three circles. The first circle includes those things about which you are passionate. What do you love to do? The second circle includes those areas in which you could be one of the best. In what areas do you have strong abilities or significant talents?

To illustrate the necessity of combining these two circles, passion and ability, let me ask you a question. Have you ever been in a situation where someone was very passionate about singing? Maybe it was a church, a karaoke bar, or the auditions for *American Idol*. The person had an obvious desire to be a great singer and clearly loved to sing. Unfortunately, she had no ability. She was awful. It was painful to watch. Have you ever experienced that? I have, and I can hardly bear the embarrassment that I feel for the other person. That is why we need to find something that includes both passion and talent. Passion is not enough.

The third circle includes those things for which you can be paid. How do you earn money now? How could you earn money by combining your passion and talent? Most people do not have the luxury of being a full-time volunteer. You have bills to pay and obligations to meet. Your mission often needs an element of financial remuneration. The intersection of these three circles is your hedgehog concept. If you can make money doing something for which you are both talented and passionate, you will find success.

John Maxwell believes that people who do what they love, even if it involves little or no pay, usually end up making a great deal of money. Their passion and ability fuel their motivation and creativity, which in turn foster financial success. In contrast, people who forsake what they love to

pursue wealth, often end up disillusioned and depressed. Their lack of enjoyment for their work stifles their motivation, and they become low performers. This, in turn, causes the loss of financial reward that they were seeking. If you are skeptical, consider the following quote from Henry David Thoreau. "I have learned this at least . . . that if one advances confidently in the direction of his dreams and endeavors to live the life he has imagined, he will meet with success unexpected in common hours."

Stephen Covey, in his book *The Eighth Habit*, adds a fourth circle to Collins' model. The fourth circle includes "conscience." He argues that you should also consider whether your hedgehog concept contributes to the world in a positive way. How can you make a difference? How can you help others?

If you want to develop or clarify your personal mission, take some time to consider the questions in each of these four circles. Create a list of activities for each and look for areas that match. You might be surprised by what you find.

I've listed a number on online tools to help you develop your mission and explore your hedgehog concept in the Factor Finder section at the end of the chapter. If you would like to recommend other related tools, please send an email to me at dave@drendall.com

I'd love to add your submission to the four factors resources on my website www.drendall.com and to future editions of the book.

### Plan

When I teach goal setting, I ask participants to share stories of failed New Year's resolutions or other goals. Everyone has a story; most have quite a few. Then I ask them about their successes. How many have successfully fulfilled a resolution? This time, only a few hands go up. What does this mean? I think it means that people are not very good at getting themselves to do what they want to do. This has significant leadership implications. If people struggle to set and achieve their own goals, then they cannot expect to inspire others to achieve mutual purposes.

There are a number of reasons why people fail to successfully implement their plans. First, they have an unclear mission. Second, they

have ambiguous goals. Third, they have conflicting priorities. Fourth, their plans are not in alignment with their true purpose.

*Ambiguous Goals*

I have already discussed the first problem and presented methods for clarifying your purpose. However, simply having a clear purpose is not enough. You need a clear strategy. Morris called this "focused concentration." You have to break your main goal into long, mid, and short term goals. One way to set better goals and have a better plan is to make sure the goals are SMART.

- Specific
- Measurable
- Achievable
- Results-Oriented
- Time-Limited

Let's use health as an example. Many people want to be healthier, but a goal to "be healthier" is not an adequate guide for action. It does not meet the first test of SMART goals. It is not *specific*. This is important because becoming healthier could mean any number of things. Eating right, exercising more, quitting smoking or drinking, wearing helmets and seatbelts, losing weight, reducing or managing stress, and getting more sleep are all potential strategies for better health.

A goal to exercise is more specific but not specific enough. Walking is one form of exercise. That will narrow it further. Now you need your goal to be *measurable*. You walk to our car each morning. You walk while shopping. Does that count? By making your goal measurable, you further clarify your intentions. Walking for thirty minutes is measurable. How often will you walk? How about three times a week?

Is this *achievable*? What is your schedule like? Do you have other obligations? Where will you walk? Does your community experience extremely cold or hot weather? Will you need equipment? These issues and others need to be addressed to determine whether a goal is achievable.

People seem to do better if they set small goals and exceed them, instead of setting high goals and falling short. If you are not exercising, a valid goal would be to walk once a week, take the stairs instead of the

elevator, or park farther away at the store. Both in our personal lives and organizations, successful changes are fostered by small wins. Success tends to motivate further success. Even small victories play a significant role in motivating us to achieve our goals and ultimately fulfill our purposes.

In my classes, I try to help students set SMART goals in their own lives. To generate discussion, we talk about failed goals from the past. One woman was trying to lose weight. Her plan was to stop eating after six o'clock each night. Many experts recommend this, since food eaten later in the evening is more readily turned into fat. She was very successful in achieving her goal. No food passed her lips after the designated time.

Unfortunately, she gained twelve pounds while supposedly achieving her goal. What happened? Her short-term goal, no eating after 6 o'clock, did not lead to the desired result, weight-loss. She found that she would wake each morning and be ravenous. She was so hungry after twelve hours of fasting that she would gorge herself between 6 a.m. and 6 p.m. each day. This story illustrates the importance of goals that are *results-oriented*. You have to ensure that your goals will lead to the desired end. Failure to do so can cause you to win the battle but lose the war.

Back to walking. The SMAR goal so far is to walk for thirty minutes, three times a week. You can walk at the mall if it is too cold or hot, and you can do it on your lunch hour. Walking is a safe form of exercise and has been shown to improve health, so your goal is results-oriented. However, you still need T, *time-limited*.

This is where a lot of people break down. If you never set a timeframe and a deadline, then you never fail to achieve our goal. You also never succeed. There is no way to truly evaluate your efforts until you know how many weeks you plan to meet your goal. When will you be done?

For example, if I set a goal to graduate from Smith College with a bachelors degree in Economics. I have a SMAR goal. Assuming that I set this goal at age 18, I now have the rest of my life to achieve it. Is that what I intended? Until I set a year or age as a deadline, I do not have a goal. I just have a general desire. If I am 40 years old and still do not have the degree, I can just tell myself that I am planning on getting my degree. I have not failed to achieve my goal. I just have not started yet. As you can see, effective goals need deadlines.

Stephen Covey, in *First Things First,* explains that most of people manage their time by focusing on what is most urgent. If something is not urgent, it tends to be neglected. Similarly, John Kotter, Harvard professor and author of *Leading Change,* argues that any successful change effort must begin by creating a sense of urgency. This is another reason that you need time-limited goals. Deadlines, even when self-imposed, create a sense of urgency that motivates action.

## Conflicting Priorities

Besides a lack of self-discipline, conflicting priorities is the most often cited reason for failing to achieve goals. People do not accomplish their goals because they are not as important or urgent as other goals. Therefore, you may not have a lack of self-discipline, you are just using it in other areas. Jim Loehr and Tony Schwartz support this idea. In *The Power of Full Engagement,* they argue that people have a limited supply of self-control and must allocate it strategically. Successful people are not necessarily more self-disciplined, they just use their allocation more wisely than unsuccessful people.

To combat the problem of conflicting priorities and ensure wise use of self-control, you need to create a comprehensive plan that accounts for all of your priorities. This involves a high degree of self-awareness, as discussed with Factor 1, Influence. People often have too narrow a view when they create goals, especially New Year's resolutions. They resolve to exercise three times a week, despite the fact that they have young children, are completing their degree, just started a new job, have overwhelming debt, and only get five hours of sleep per night. The priorities of family, education, work, adequate sleep, and financial stability must be addressed when devising any new goals. This can be accomplished in the *achievable* section of the SMART goal process.

## Lack of Alignment

The final barrier to goal achievement is lack of alignment between your goals and your purpose. This is similar to what was discussed in the section on results-oriented goals. However, it requires additional clarification. People sometimes set goals in areas that they do not truly value. There are many reasons for this, usually related to pressure from others and a desire to fulfill others' expectations. People also fail to be honest with themselves about what they value. Again, this is sometimes due to relationships with people who do not share their values. Other times they

are simply unaware of their values, and they have not identified their priorities. This further reinforces the importance of intentionally developing self-awareness.

### *Passion*

People's actions are driven more strongly by their feelings than their thoughts. Leaders must connect with people's emotions because their hearts regularly overrule their heads. This is why Tom Morris says that one of the seven conditions of success is "emotional commitment." He cites Plato's strategy for persuasion which included logos (thought), pathos (emotion) and ethos (integrity). Pathos is important because knowledge is not sufficient to motivate action. Have you ever heard someone say, "I don't feel like it?" Their feelings were guiding their decision.

Social psychologists Marie Helweg-Larsen and Barry Collins studied people's responses to information regarding AIDS prevention. They found that information alone did not lead people to change their behavior. People know what to do, but for various reasons, they do not feel like doing what they know is right. This reluctance is usually related to the awkward relational and emotional situations that would result from discussing AIDS testing, requiring their partner to use a condom, or inquiring about past sexual relationships. For people to change their behavior, they need to deal with the emotional consequences of that change.

Daniel Goleman supported this emphasis on emotional appeal. He cited research that people who lost functioning in the emotional part of their brain also lost the ability to make decisions. They do not have preferences any more because their choices no longer have emotional consequences. Their minds can still reason through the options, but they have no impetus for making a decision.

Effective leaders recognize this reality, and they attempt to speak to people's *hearts* as well as their *heads*, two critical elements of the *H3* model. Economist John Kenneth Galbraith claimed that "all of the great leaders have had one characteristic in common: it was the willingness to confront unequivocally the major anxiety of their people in their time. This, and not much else, is the essence of leadership." This reinforces the importance of empathy, discussed in Factor 1. Leaders must understand their follower's hopes, dreams, and fears before they can touch their hearts.

The importance of passion is even more important when encountering barriers to achieving the vision.

### Perseverance

Markita needed to overcome her shyness in order to fulfill her purpose. Melissa did not get help from President Bush, but that did not stop her. She pursued other options before she received a reply. It also did not discourage her from approaching famous and powerful people, as evidenced by her subsequent letter to Sam Walton.

Achieving your mission is not easy. It requires the ability to delay gratification. You need to be able to endure the discomfort that comes with waiting for that second marshmallow. As Tom Morris explains, people need a "stubborn consistency" as they encounter obstacles. This illustrates how the four factors build on each other. Your ability to persevere will require significant self-discipline, Factor 1, and the confidence that comes from making and keeping promises to yourself, Factor 2. Your ability to overcome obstacles is also related to the strength of your purpose, Factor 3. In discussing the importance of meaning and purpose, Victor Frankl cited Nietzsche's declaration that "he who has a why, can withstand any how."

It is relatively easy to make plans, but it can be very difficult to carry them out. In 2004, I decided to run a marathon. This was significant since my only exercise for the previous eight years included an occasional round of golf. My purpose was clear. I would complete the Myrtle Beach Marathon on February 19, 2005.

Plans for marathon training are readily available, and there is little equipment required. There were plenty of resources related to nutrition, clothing, and proper footwear. I knew when to run and for how long. That was the easy part. The difficult part was running. It required me to make time in my schedule. It required me to endure physical pain and exhaustion. I had to run in rain, heat, and cold. The day of the race brought temperatures of 27 degrees. Ultimately, achieving my goal and completing my plan meant I had to actually run 26.2 miles, which took more than four hours.

Like running a marathon, fulfilling your mission will not be easy, but it can be tremendously rewarding. As I trained for the marathon I lost thirty pounds and gained an incredible amount of energy. I changed to healthier eating habits and felt much better than I had before taking on this

challenge. When you persevere in the pursuit of your mission, it may not be easy, but it will be worth it.

## Interpersonal Dimension
### *Vision*

Kouzes and Posner propose "inspiring a shared vision" as one of the five exemplary practices of a leader. This practice includes "envisioning an uplifting and ennobling future" and "enlisting others in a common vision by appealing to their values, interests, hopes, and dreams." Leadership is a relationship based on influence and integrity, but leadership also implies movement. Vision sets a goal and a destination. Vision provides a focus for influence and the leadership relationship.

As Markita, Tommy, and Melissa illustrated, leaders first develop a personal vision. They then create progress. As they move consistently toward that vision, they find followers. Leadership happens on the journey. Bennis and Nanus argued that inspiring a shared vision requires a demonstration of a personal commitment to the destination. People will not follow a leader who is *bringing up the rear*. Peter Drucker contended that too many lives were lost in World War I because "not enough generals were killed." They were too far from the battle and did not understand what they were asking people to do.

The movie *We Were Soldiers* presents a contrasting style of military leadership. In this true story of the first major cavalry engagement of the Vietnam War, Lieutenant Colonel Hal Moore gives the following speech to his troops before they leave their base in the United States.

> We are going into battle against a tough and determined enemy. I cannot promise you that I will bring you all home alive. But this I swear . . . when we go into battle, *I will be the first to step on the field and I will be the last to step off.* And I will leave no one behind . . . dead or alive. We will all come home together.

Leaders show their commitment to the vision by being the first on and the last off the field of battle. In addition to leading by example, it is also necessary to explicitly share your personal mission or vision. Inspiring a shared vision involves other forms of verbal explanation and persuasion.

If there is no vision, there is no need for a leader. Influence and integrity have no meaningful object without an inspiring vision. Mark Sanborn said that leadership is an "invitation to greatness." People want their leaders to motivate them and to help them believe that they can be greater than they are and that the world can be better than it is. This is evident in the effectiveness of Martin Luther King Jr.'s *I Have a Dream* speech and Winston Churchill's inspiring radio addresses during World War II. Quinn argues that leaders "find, develop, evaluate, and communicate a vision that will move others to their highest levels of excellence." Leaders can communicate their vision by painting a *picture* of an *ideal future reality*.

### *Picture*

The word vision evokes the idea of sight. Effective leaders use pictures and images to clearly communicate their vision. They use vivid images to illustrate their ideas. They color in the painting with detailed explanations of how the world could be. It has been said that "a picture is worth a thousand words." Those who use words effectively know how to use them to create pictures in the minds of their listeners.

In *How to Learn a Foreign Language*, Graham Fuller suggests that students connect the words of a different language with a picture of the object they represent. This is more memorable than trying to associate the foreign word with the word from one's native language. Our minds respond to the power of images.

Furthermore, social psychologist David Myers argues that the vividness of pictures and experiences affect people's response. In other words, more vivid images take precedence over those with less color and detail. Therefore, leaders must seek to be both as precise and as lavish as possible in describing their vision. This is why Martin Luther King Jr. used phrases like "the red hills of Georgia" in his famous, *I Have a Dream* speech.

Stories and metaphors are also excellent methods for vividly sharing a vision. Before written language was developed or widely used, people used stories to make the spoken word more memorable. Stories still provide an excellent method for communicating a compelling vision. Daniel Pink, in *A Whole New Mind,* contends that the effective use of story is one of six aptitudes that will be essential for success in the future.

Metaphors involve using something already known to illustrate something that is unknown or not clearly understood. This is especially important since vision implies something different from that which currently exists. For example, Martin Luther King Jr. used the metaphor of banking to explain inadequacy of existing civil rights legislation. He explained that black Americans had been written a check that they could not cash. There were insufficient funds. This metaphor crystallized and united myriad problems into one clear picture. A picture of a person who had not received what they were owed. A person who had been denied what was rightly theirs. Just like this person, like any reasonable person in a society of law and order, black Americans wanted justice.

### *Ideal*

A vision promotes a picture that is better than current circumstances. It describes what could and should be. Vision capitalizes on the power of expectancy. For people to act in a certain way, they must believe that their act will lead to a valued reward. A vision must connect with people's actual needs and values. Whether or not a vision meets the test of being ideal is determined by potential followers, not the leader. This again reinforces the importance of empathy, understanding others.

A compelling vision offers a positive alternative to existing reality. It calms people's fears and gives them hope that tomorrow will be better than today. For example, another source of power in the *I Have a Dream* speech was the fact that the dream was ideal for so many people. The oppression of black citizens was inexcusable. Many lived in constant danger and fear. This negative reality was sharply contrasted with the dream, with what could and should be, with the potential for change and improvement. In the dream, good triumphed over evil.

Leaders also remind people of the significance of the vision. They provide a larger context for the particular goal. This is illustrated by the following story. A man was walking along the road when he encountered three men laying bricks. He asked them what they were doing and received three very different responses. The first man said that he was laying bricks. The second man said that he was building a wall. The third man said that he was building a cathedral. Which man saw the significance of his work? Tom Morris argued that "any job, productive of any good, can have either a noble or a trivial description." He called this the "dual significance principle." Similarly, Daniel Pink argues that, in an age of increasing

abundance, people want more than just survival, they long for meaning. Leaders help people to see the nobility of their work. They bring meaning to people's lives.

However, some situations might seem to be devoid of potentially positive visions. Some tasks may not seem glorious, but effective leaders find and communicate their glory. C. William Pollard is the former CEO of ServiceMaster. One of the primary activities of his firm was janitorial services. This might not seem noble or inherently uplifting, but Pollard was able to inspire his employees with a vision for their organization.

In 1968, shortly before he was assassinated, Martin Luther King Jr. spoke to a crowd of over 15,000 people in Memphis. The purpose of his speech was to encourage the city's striking sanitation workers. However, listening to the speech, it was not obvious that he was addressing people who collected garbage. As the strike clearly demonstrated, garbage disposal was a vital task. King found the nobility in the job and communicated it passionately to his crowd. The white officials of the city wanted to promote a trivial description of the job, but King was more persuasive. Effective leaders can create a positive and uplifting image of their vision, even in seemingly ordinary circumstances.

### *Future Reality*
A vision paints a picture of an ideal world that does not yet exist. Visions are not focused on reality, except as a contrast to the ideal picture. Jonathan Swift stated that "vision is the art of seeing the invisible." Designing a vision requires imagination and creativity. It involves the ability to conceive of a place that you have never been or circumstances you have never experienced. Furthermore, it is necessary to describe this surreal destination in vivid detail.

Although you have never been there, and you do not know for sure what it will be like, your destination, your vision, must have an element of reality. It has to be believable. It must seem possible. That does not mean that it will be easy; leaders need perseverance. However, people will not persevere if they believe the goal is unattainable. Remember expectancy theory. For people to take action, they must believe that they have the ability to do what is required. Without meeting the first condition, elements of reward are irrelevant. The vision must be challenging but possible. This is a delicate balance.

King understood this balance. For all the majesty of the *Dream* speech, one of the lines, intermixed with visions of peace and harmony, was "we will go to jail together." He had a beautiful dream of love and justice, but the path to the dream would be guarded by hate and injustice. This was an accurate portrayal, as evidenced by King's own violent death, and many would argue that his dream, the shared dream of millions of black Americans, has not yet been fulfilled.

This illustrates the power of King's words. He convinced people that the dream, though unlikely, was worth pursuing. That is the burden of visionary leaders, to convince people that the vision is possible, even when it is potentially impossible. A vision is a picture of an ideal future reality. King was a master at painting that picture.

## Factor Figure
### *Dr. Martin Luther King Jr.*

Dr. King personified inspiration. He had a powerful sense of personal mission and believed he was called to lead his people out of oppression. His words rallied millions of people to join the cause of justice for black Americans. He gave courage to people who had been discouraged and hope to people who were hopeless.

King also demonstrated significant perseverance as he pursued his vision. He spent time in jail on a number of occasions. In fact, his book *Letters from a Birmingham Jail,* had a profound impact on the civil rights movement in America. His house was bombed, and he received constant death threats. During one march in the South, he was struck in the head with a brick and he was stabbed during a book signing in New York. Finally, he was killed because of his commitment to the cause of liberty. He was willing to endure imprisonment, physical abuse, and death to fulfill his vision. His life and violent death are a testimony to the power of inspiration.

## Factor Failure
### *Josef Stalin*

Josef Stalin ruled Russia with an iron fist for more than a quarter century. During that time, he used his position to deify himself and oppress his people. His vision was neither shared by his people nor ideal for the majority of Russian citizens. His policies are blamed for famines that led to the deaths of millions. Instead of inspiring people with a compelling vision, he relied on his status as Russia's formal ruler to legitimize his actions.

For nearly 30 years, he attempted to silence the voices of all who opposed him. This involved censorship, murder, deportation and imprisonment that destroyed the lives of millions of individuals and their families. Despite widespread discontent, he engineered ubiquitous public and private monuments to himself, which supposedly demonstrated that he was loved and revered by his people.

The extent to which he propagated this myth gave rise to the term *cult of personality*. This is defined by Wikipedia as a "political institution in which a country's leader encourages praise of himself and his deeds to such a degree that this praise affects nearly every facet of the country's culture." Other destructive perpetuators of the cult of personality were Iraq's Saddam Hussein, Romania's Nicolae Ceausescu, and Italy's Benito Mussolini. This concept encompasses elements of the factor fiction from each chapter. These pseudo-leaders relied on power instead of influence, personality instead of integrity, position instead of inspiration, and popularity instead of improvement.

## Factor Fiction
### *Position*

Instead of recognizing the importance of vision, many believe that leadership is primarily a position. This is the belief that supervisors, managers, and CEOs are leaders and that leadership is the result of authority, rank or title, not a picture of an ideal future reality. If someone wants to become a leader, then she needs to get hired or promoted to a leadership position. French and Raven refer to position as "legitimate power."

This belief causes many people to give up on the idea of becoming a leader. Believing that leadership is a position eliminates the majority of people from potential leadership. A lot of the people in my classes and seminars believe that they cannot be leaders because they do not have, and might never attain, a managerial position.

This is not to say that someone with management responsibilities cannot be a leader. However, position is not a requirement for leadership. Reuter contended that "leadership is the result of an ability to persuade or direct men, *apart from the prestige or power that comes from office* or other external circumstances." This belief was confirmed by leadership speaker and author Robin Sharma. "Leadership is not about the prestige of your title

but the quality of your character. Real leadership is not about position, it's about action."

In fact, a concern for position actually seems to actually impede the development of true leadership. A review of the lives of Hitler, Stalin and others quickly reveals the lengths to which people will go to obtain and maintain their positions. In contrast, many of the greatest leaders in the world had no formal organizational or political position.

For example, former president Jimmy Carter's administration was marked by turmoil and discord. By many accounts, he struggled to lead in his position as president. In contrast, he has been tremendously influential in his volunteer work with Habitat for Humanity. This suggests that leadership is not a position. Instead, leadership is the process of inspiring a shared vision.

Effective leaders have a strong personal mission. They also have the plan, passion, and perseverance to accomplish their mission. Their example draws others to them, and they have the opportunity to inspire a shared vision. This is accomplished by painting a vivid picture of an ideal future reality. To achieve this vision, leaders constantly learn and grow and develop those around them. This is the subject of Factor 4, *Improvement*.

## Factor Focus

1. What is your personal mission?
2. Why don't most people take the time to develop their mission?
3. Kouzes and Posner's research shows that people admire those who are forward-looking. Do you spend more of your time looking back at the past, around at present circumstances, or looking ahead? Why?
4. What are some ways that you could improve your ability to look ahead?
5. Do you see yourself as an inspirational person? Why or why not?
6. What are you passionate about?
7. Which is the most important?
   - Having a clear purpose
   - Having a plan
   - Having passion
   - Persevering
8. How could you paint a picture of an ideal future reality?

9. What are some ways that you could inspire a shared vision without using words?
10. What is a noble description of your work?
11. What is a trivial description of your work?
12. How could you communicate the nobility of your work to others?
13. Why do we often rely on position instead of inspiration?
14. What are the consequences of relying on position?

## Factor Future
1. Read a biography of Martin Luther King Jr. and/or watch the A&E Biography.
2. Read selected books from the *factor facts* section.
3. Complete the self-assessments in the *factor finder* section.
4. Discover your personal hedgehog concept.
5. Develop a personal mission statement.
6. Develop a vision for a group/team project.

## Factor Finder
*Developing Your Personal Mission*
http://www.jimcollins.com/lab/hedgehog/index.html
- Explains the hedgehog concept and has audio lessons to help with application.

http://www.franklincovey.com/fc/library_and_resources/mission_statement_builder
- Good explanation of the mission development process and helpful interactive tool.

http://www.quintcareers.com/mission_statements.html
- Good introduction to the mission development process and links to other resources.

http://www.quintcareers.com/mission_statement_exercises.html
- Good questions and exercises to get you started.

http://www.quintcareers.com/mission_statement_development.html
- More exercises and questions.

http://www.quintcareers.com/creating_personal_mission_statements.html
- Five-step process for developing your mission

http://www.fastcompany.com/magazine/13/ldrplus.html
- Article with excellent tips for mission development

http://www.nightingale.com/tMission_PersonalStatement.asp
- Good overview and development tools. Requires email address to begin.

*Inspiring a Shared Vision*
http://www.1000ventures.com/business_guide/crosscuttings/vision_mission_strategy.html
- Good overview and tips for developing a company vision, mission and strategy

http://www.tgci.com/magazine/98fall/mission.asp
- Guidelines for writing a mission that apply to nonprofit and for-profit organizations

http://www.managementhelp.org/plan_dec/str_plan/str_plan.htm
- A treasure trove of articles and links related to strategy development

http://top7business.com/?Top-7-Tips-for-Creating-an-Inspiring-Vision&id=573

*Various*
http://www.mhhe.com/business/management/buildyourmanagementskills/menu.html
Select "self-assessments"
- *Communication Style*
- *Creativity*

*Leadership Practices Inventory*
http://www.lpionline.com/lpi/
Based on Kouzes and Posner's Leadership Challenge (requires survey administration and purchase of license)
- *Inspire a Shared Vision*

*21 Irrefutable Laws of Leadership*
http://www.injoy.com/OnlineTools/assessment.aspx
Based on John Maxwell's book with the same title
21 different assessments for each leadership law
Requires free, brief online registration (email address, name, zipcode)

*- Navigation: Anyone can steer the ship, but it takes a leader to chart the course*
*- Priorities: Leaders understand that activity isn't necessarily accomplishment*

*17 Indisputable Laws of Teamwork*
http://www.injoy.com/OnlineTools/assessment.aspx
Based on John Maxwell's book with the same title
17 different assessments for each teamwork law
Requires free, brief online registration (email address, name, zipcode)
*- Big Picture: The goal is more important than the role*
*- Compass: Vision gives team members direction and confidence*
*- Communication: Interaction fuels action*

### Factor Facts

Frankl                                      *Man's Search for Meaning*
- The ultimate book on developing a meaningful purpose. Powerful story, insightful principles.

Jones                                       *The Path*

Leider                                      *The Power of Purpose*

Phillips                                    *Martin Luther King, Jr. on Leadership*
- Learn about inspiration from the life of one of the world's greatest leaders.

| Factor | Foundation |
|---|---|
| **Bass** <br> *Leadership and Performance Beyond Expectation* <br><br><br> **Burns** <br> *Leadership* | Transformational Leadership <br> - Inspirational Motivation |
| **Bennis & Nanus** <br> *Leaders* | Four Strategies <br> - Attention through Vision <br> - Meaning through Communication |
| **Covey** <br> *The Seven Habits of Highly Effective People* | Seven Habits <br> - Habit 2: Begin with the End in Mind <br> - Habit 3: Put First Things First |
| **Collins** <br> *Good to Great* | The Hedgehog Concept |
| **Finzel** <br> *The Top Ten Mistakes Leaders Make* | Top Ten Mistakes <br> - Communication Chaos <br> - Failure to Focus on the Future |
| **Kouzes & Posner** <br> *The Leadership Challenge* | Five Exemplary Practices <br> - Inspire a Shared Vision <br> - Challenge the Process |
| **Maxwell** <br> *The 21 Irrefutable Laws of Leadership* | 21 Irrefutable Laws <br> - Navigation: Anyone can steer the ship, but it takes a leader to chart the course <br> - Priorities: Leaders understand that activity isn't necessarily accomplishment |

| | |
|---|---|
| *The 21 Indispensable Qualities of a Leader* | <u>21 Indispensable Qualities</u><br>- Communication: Without it, you travel alone<br>- Focus: The sharper it is, the sharper you are<br>- Vision: You can only seize what you can see<br>- Commitment: It separates the dreamers from the doers<br>- Passion: Take this life and love it |
| **Morris**<br>*True Success*<br>*The Art of Achievement* | <u>Seven Cs of Success</u><br>- Commitment<br>- Conception<br>- Concentration |
| **Senge**<br>*The Fifth Discipline* | <u>Five Disciplines</u><br>- Shared Vision |

# Factor Quotient
## *Inspiration*

Please read each of the statements listed below.
Record your level of agreement with each statement in the blank to the left.
Total your answers and refer to the scoring key at the end of the assessment.

*5 Strongly Agree   4 Agree   3 Not Sure   2 Disagree   1 Strongly Disagree*

---

| | | |
|---|---|---|
| _____ | 1. | I demonstrate perseverance when encountering obstacles. |
| _____ | 2. | I regularly achieve my goals. |
| _____ | 3. | I have a written mission statement for my life. |
| _____ | 4. | I am passionate about my purpose. |
| _____ | 5. | I have clear priorities. |
| _____ | 6. | My actions are in alignment with my priorities. |
| _____ | 7. | I set SMART goals. |
| _____ | 8. | When formulating my vision, I consider the hopes and dreams of others. |
| _____ | 9. | When sharing my vision, I appeal to people's hearts and minds. |
| _____ | 10. | I clearly and consistently communicate my vision to others. |

_____ **Total Score**

## Scoring Key
**41-50**  Great, maximize your abilities in this factor
**31-40**  Good, continue to fine-tune certain aspects of this factor
**21-30**  You may want to focus attention on this factor
**< 26**  This factor might be a barrier to your leadership effectiveness

# Factor 4
## *Improvement*

Live as if you were to die tomorrow. Learn as if you were to live forever.

- Mahatma Gandhi

Keep away from people who belittle your ambitions. Small people always do that, but the really great make you feel that you too can become great.

- Mark Twain

I start with the premise that the function of leadership is to produce more leaders, not more followers.

- Ralph Nader

### Factor Feat
#### *Bill Walsh*

Bill Walsh is the former head coach for the San Francisco 49ers football team. During his nine-year tenure, the team won three Super Bowls and six NFC Western Division titles. He was named Coach of the Year in 1981 and 1984, and Coach of the Decade for the 1980s. He was also inducted into the NFL Hall of Fame. However, none of these accomplishments represent his true greatness. His status as one of the greatest football coaches of all time is related to his ability to develop other leaders.

Ten of Walsh's former assistant coaches became head coaches for other NFL teams, and they have had tremendous success in their new positions. George Seifert won two Super Bowls after taking the reins of the 49ers from Walsh. The Denver Broncos also won two Super Bowls while Mike Shanahan was their head coach. Mike Holmgren won the Super Bowl

with the Green Bay Packers in 1996. The Baltimore Ravens won their first Super Bowl in 2000, with Brian Billick at the helm, but the story does not end there.

Walsh's former assistants learned about more than just football while working for him. After becoming head coaches, they also spawned new head coaches and Super Bowl champions. For example, John Gruden led the Tampa Bay Buccaneers to a Super Bowl win in 2002 after working for three different Walsh assistants, Holmgren, Rhodes, and Siefert. Nearly 15 years after Walsh left the NFL, the leaders he developed were still dominating the sport.

How does this compare to other successful coaches? Bill Parcells won two Super Bowls during his coaching career, while Joe Gibbs and Jimmy Johnson each won three. Dan Reeves coached in two Super Bowls and Marv Levy led his team to four, but neither coach won any of those games. No other coach even comes close to matching Walsh's ability to develop others leaders who could duplicate his success.

Taken together, former assistants to Parcells, Gibbs, Johnson, Reeves, and Levy account for just 4 Super Bowl wins and 7 appearances. In comparison, the leaders Walsh developed have won 7 Super Bowls and participated in 11. Walsh's numbers would have been even more impressive, but only one team can win the championship each year. In 2002, when Gruden's Buccaneers won the Super Bowl, they defeated the Oakland Raiders, who were coached by another Walsh descendant, Bill Callahan.

Walsh's career illustrates at least two important leadership principles. First, leaders are learners. They learn about themselves, others, and the world around them. They learn for a lifetime. Second, leaders take what they have learned and become teachers and facilitators. They teach both explicitly, through words and lessons, and implicitly, by modeling the attitudes and behaviors they hope to foster. They also create environments that facilitate learning.

Effective leaders have learned that the vision cannot be accomplished alone. Because of this, they focus on helping their followers to be successful. Max DePree supports this view, when he argues that leadership is "enabling others to reach their potential." Similarly, former

U.S. Senator and NBA Hall of Famer Bill Bradley believes that "leadership is unlocking people's potential to become better." Covey and others refer to this as empowerment.

Furthermore, effective leaders do not just develop followers. They also produce new leaders. This is reinforced by the familiar leadership maxim "there is no success without a successor."

### Internal Dimension
### *Self-Development*

Nathaniel Greene was one of the most influential American generals during the Revolutionary War. With no previous military experience, he read every book he could find on warfare and leadership. His willingness to teach himself and learn from his mistakes allowed him to become an effective leader in the midst of a dangerous and immensely challenging situation. Historian David McCullough explained that, because of his willingness to learn, Greene became one of George Washington's most trusted advisors.

Similarly, Abraham Lincoln's success was largely related to his self-education. Lincoln taught himself how to read and write, and he made extraordinary efforts to get access to books, often walking for miles to secure new reading material. Donald Phillips wrote that "he so dramatically increased his ability to speak and write that he is today regarded as a model for poetic and artistic expression." His legal education involved traveling long distances on foot to the courthouse to observe the sessions. Even while President, he was a patient and attentive listener, recognizing that he could learn from those around him.

### *Leaders are Learners*

There are many different ways to learn. However, there is strong evidence that effective leaders are voracious readers. In an age before it was understood that people have different learning styles, Mark Twain proclaimed that "a person who won't read has no advantage over one who can't read." Even if you do not enjoy reading, there is no excuse for not pursuing some type of self-development. I will explore different learning strategies below.

*Reading*

Reading is one of the easiest and most accessible ways to learn. Effective leaders expand their knowledge by reading books, relevant magazines and journals, newspapers, and websites. The internet is a tremendous resource for information on any subject, including leadership.

When I was working on my doctorate, I did not have time to read anything other than my course textbooks. This led me to another great learning strategy, audio books. This is what Zig Ziglar calls "automobile university." I spend many hours in the car driving to work and to various speaking engagements. I have been able to listen to at least one book each week during my commute.

The car is not the only place to listen to audio books. While training for marathons and triathlons, I listen to audio books using a portable tape, CD, or mp3 player. I knew that my first marathon might get a little dull after four hours on the road, so I downloaded an audio book to my mp3 player. Unfortunately, the book was finished long before I was.

---

If you or someone you know would like to enroll in automobile university, go to www.drendall.com and order one or more of the following audio seminars available in CD or mp3. Each seminar includes PowerPoint slides and notes that can be downloaded directly from the website.

- GROW! Ten Strategies for Maximizing your Leadership Potential.
- RECHARGE! Managing Stress through Personal Renewal
- CREATE! Leading by Initiating Change and Inventing the Future

- THE FOUR FACTORS OF EFFECTIVE LEADERSHIP
    - Live Seminar
    - Unabridged Audiobook

---

One of the strengths and weaknesses of reading is that it is largely a self-directed and solitary activity. In contrast, seminars and formal education can provide more structure and social contact for learning. These options can take a number of different forms: one-day training sessions, major conferences, certificate programs, and higher education degrees. Each

person needs to decide what is appropriate for her needs. Each medium has merit, and I would recommend a combination.

### Finding a Mentor

An even more personal and relational method of learning is to be mentored. Having a mentor allows you to address specific needs and receive advice and support from someone with relevant knowledge and experiences. The obvious advantage of this approach is the tailored nature of the learning and the relationship that develops in the process. Many leaders have more than one mentor, with each person guiding them in a particular area.

### Being a Mentor

It can be a tremendous learning experience to be a mentor. When you help another person, you have the opportunity to reflect on your existing knowledge and experiences. Mentoring can also motivate you to learn more. To provide assistance, you often need resources that you do not already possess. Your responsibility as a mentor provides the impetus to seek out new knowledge.

You can also learn from the persons you are mentoring. Inevitably they will have unique and valuable perspectives on issues that are relevant to you. You should not see mentoring as a one-way relationship. It can provide mutual benefits. Finally, as you share what you have learned, you learn it again and usually come to understand it in a deeper way.

### Teaching

Teaching is valuable for a similar reason. Covey goes so far as to argue that people do not truly understand something until they can clearly explain it to someone else. For this reason, many trainers and speakers encourage participants to choose one relevant concept to teach to others when they return to their home or office.

### Research

Research is yet another way to learn. Leaders often encounter situations that require difficult decisions or require knowledge that they do not possess. Effective leaders know how to find, analyze, and synthesize different sources of information and use what they have learned to make better decisions, solve problems, or develop plans. As I like to tell my students, "life is an open book test." You are not measured so much by what

you already know as by your ability to locate and learn relevant information when it is needed. The advantage of this learning strategy is that it is more integrated into daily activities than others.

*Listen*

Listening is an often neglected method of learning. However, as Lincoln demonstrated, it can be very powerful. It does not require you to do any more than give your sincere attention to the person who is speaking. Unfortunately, people are usually too busy talking or thinking about what they are going to say next, to truly listen. The importance of listening is reinforced by Covey's habit "seek first to understand and then to be understood" and Goleman's emphasis on empathy.

*Experiences*

A final strategy is to actively seek out new and different experiences. These can include challenging projects, foreign travel, adventure trips, or volunteer work. Virtually any situation is a potential learning experience. However, you do not necessarily learn automatically. It is helpful to reflect and try to make sense of what you have experienced. Keeping a journal is one strategy that many leaders have successfully employed to assist them in this process. This section discussed strategies for learning. Next, I will examine areas on which to focus your educational efforts, as well as a rationale for each area.

### What to Learn, Why to Learn it

President John F. Kennedy believed that "leadership and learning are indispensable to each other." That is true for a number of reasons. These are illustrated by each of the four factors, which provide a focus for self-development.

Factor 1, *Influence*, demonstrated the need for self-awareness, understanding self, and empathy, understanding others. Your ability to control yourself is directly related to your self-knowledge. Therefore, leaders need to continually learn more about their thoughts, feelings, motivations, values, strengths, interests, fears, and weaknesses. They also need to understand the connection between their head, heart, and hands. This was illustrated by the *H3* model. Your ability to influence others is also tied to your knowledge of others. Leaders must know their followers almost as well as they know themselves.

Factor 2, *Integrity*, discussed the need for competence. This means that you need to learn about leadership and the particular arena in which you lead. You also need to develop and improve your abilities in these areas.

Factor 3, *Inspiration*, reinforced the necessity of communicating a shared vision. In order to do this effectively, you need to know what followers desire and what they fear. You need to understand their values and goals. One of the first principles of effective speaking is to know your audience. As you try to inspire others to pursue the vision, knowledge of your audience is absolutely essential.

Factor 3 also involves developing a personal mission and a picture of an ideal future reality. To do this more effectively, it is worthwhile to study trends and seek out information that will help you to anticipate the future. There are various books and magazines devoted to this subject. Although you cannot control the future, you can often predict it with reasonable certainty. A good example of this process is meteorology. Weather forecasters do not control the weather and they are not always right, but people still watch their predictions because it helps them to prepare for what might happen.

One final area for learning encompasses all of the factors because it influences the way that people process information. The following story illustrates this concept. One night I was talking with my sister. I do not remember what we were talking about, but I do remember that we were sitting no more than three feet apart. At one point she seemed to be distracted, and I asked her what she was doing. She continued to look at my feet and then asked me if I was wearing socks. This seemed like an odd question since we were sitting so close and my feet were in plain view. I told her that I was wearing socks, but I was still confused by her inability to see. She could not see because it was later in the evening, and she had taken out her contacts. She had not bothered to put on her glasses since she was going to bed soon. Her vision was so poor that without her glasses, everything was shaded and blurry.

Just like my sister, our minds use glasses to see the world. Without your glasses, you cannot make sense of the information that you find. This is why people use the phrase "looking through rose-colored glasses." The phrase implies that someone is not seeing things as they truly are. Instead,

her vision is colored or affected by glasses. This distortion of vision is also evident in the warning on the side-view mirrors in many cars. "Objects in the mirror are closer than they appear." In others words, what you see does not perfectly match reality. The point is that the *ways* we see affect *what* we see.

These glasses or lenses can be described in different ways. Peter Senge calls them mental models. Covey refers to them as paradigms. Bolman and Deal call them frames. Another helpful analogy is to think of them as maps. Accurate maps enable you to reach your destination. Inaccurate maps cause you to be confused and disoriented. Therefore, it is important to make sure that your maps are accurate, that your glasses have the right prescription.

This means that you need to recognize the fact that you have glasses. You then need to take them off and look at them. You need to consider their strengths and weaknesses. You need to examine whether or not they are distorting your view. This is what psychologists call meta-cognition, thinking about your thinking. You need to become aware of not just *what* you think, but *how* you think.

### *Continuous Learning*
Mike Krzyzewski is the head coach of Duke University's men's basketball team. He has led his teams to eight Final Four appearances and back-to-back national championships in 1991 and 1992. His players have one of the highest graduation rates in the NCAA. In his book *Leading with the Heart*, he made a strong argument for the importance of personal growth.

> Continual learning is the key to effective leadership because no one can know everything there is to know. In leadership, things change, events change, circumstances change, people change. As a matter of fact, leadership is all about change. Leaders take people to places they've never been before. Because leaders are always encountering new situations, they have to learn how to meet new challenges, to adapt, to confront, to master, to win. A leader's job is ongoing . . . Leadership never stops. We have to think of ways to learn and grow every day because when you stop growing you start to decay.

Mahatma Gandhi encouraged others to "live as if you were to die tomorrow. Learn as if you were to live forever." This is good advice. Although learning will not help you live forever, learning might actually help you live a longer, more satisfying life. Psychologists and doctors have found that people who continue to learn into their later years have a lower incidence of dementia and Alzheimer's disease. Minds works like muscles, when you use them, they grow stronger, but if you neglect them, they die.

Continuous learning requires an attitude of humility. This is one of the characteristics of the "Level 5 leaders" described by Collins. When you learn, you acknowledge that you do not know everything there is to know. You acknowledge your limitations. This is uncomfortable for some people, and many simply rely on past learning.

Continuous learning also means that personal growth is not an activity separate from the rest of life. Each moment of each day offers learning opportunities. Philosopher John Dewey believed that "education is not preparation for life; education is life itself." This is the theory behind Peter Senge's concept of the learning organization. He argued that, like effective individuals, successful organizations were constantly gaining new knowledge.

There are many limitations to the practice of separating learning from action. In an effort to combat these problems, many companies have adopted a policy of just-in-time training, which offers learning opportunities immediately before employees will be expected to perform new skills. This is in contrast to the traditional practice of extensive employee orientation and academic style seminars.

Noel Tichy pioneered the strategy of action learning through his work with leadership development at General Electric. Action learning requires students to analyze an existing issue within the company, design a plan of action, and implement their plan. This process is facilitated by an advisor who helps participants to learn from their experiences, including mistakes and failures.

### Balance & Renewal
So far, this section has focused on learning and development. However, effective leaders also recognize the need to balance growth and renewal, action and rest. Loehr and Schwartz, authors of *The Power of Full*

*Engagement*, argue that "We must learn to live our lives as a series of sprints – fully engaged for period of time – and then fully disengaged and seeking renewal."

Leadership is focused on achieving meaningful goals. Because of this, leaders are often tempted to do too much, for too long, with too little. However, in order to achieve those goals, there is a need to balance energy expenditure with energy renewal. This does not mean doing less. Rather, it means doing things in such a way as to achieve maximum results.

Loehr and Schwartz encourage people to discover "recovery rituals" that help develop a more appropriate integration of internal needs and external demands. Recovery rituals are simply habits that make renewal a routine part of life. They believe that "The number of hours in a day is fixed, but the quantity and quality of energy available . . . is not." Rituals allow people to maximize their energy and their effectiveness. Covey calls this balancing productivity with production capacity. Some activities help us to get things done, while other activities enhance our ability to get things done in the future.

Covey explains that many people neglect energy renewal because "maintenance seldom pays dramatic, immediate dividends." However, the long term benefits of consistent rest and renewal are significant. Below are a number of suggestions for renewing energy and enhancing your production capacity in four dimensions of your life: physical, social/emotional, mental, and spiritual.

- *Physical*
    o Nutrition
    o Exercise
    o Rest

- *Mental*
    o Formal education
    o Reading
    o Reflecting on experiences
    o Listening
    o Continuous learning

- *Social/Emotional*
  - o Empathy
  - o Relationships
  - o Listening
  - o Serving others
  - o Trust account deposits

- *Spiritual*
  - o Prayer
  - o Meditation
  - o Nature
  - o Great literature
  - o Inspiring music

Most experts suggest spending at least one hour per day on personal renewal. This may seem difficult at first, but have faith that this time is not being wasted. It is an investment that will pay strong dividends. Evidence for this can be found in my experience as a marathon runner.

Many running gurus promote the importance of recovery as a part of both training and racing. For example, most long-distance runners will run for as long as they can, and then stop when they get too tired. This seems to make sense and it is one way to build endurance. However, it is actually more beneficial to combine running with short walking breaks. Changing running speeds can also accomplish the same effect. This enables the runner to go farther and exercise longer, thus building greater endurance.

Similarly, many marathon runners incorporate walking into their actual race plan. For example, I walk for one minute every two miles. This enables me to drink fluids and allows my muscles just enough rest to help me come back even stronger. Studies have shown that these walking breaks can actually decrease your final time. This is certainly counterintuitive but it is a concrete, physical example of the power of renewal.

---

If you'd like to learn more about personal renewal, go to www.drendall.com and order RECHARGE! Managing Stress through Personal Renewal. Available in 60-minute Audio CD.

---

It is clear that effective leaders are continuous learners. They use a variety of methods to learn about themselves, others, and the world around them. They are in a constant state of growth and development and they devote sufficient time to personal renewal. However, as with the other factors, it does not end there.

In the words of Guy Kawasaki, leaders should "eat like a bird, poop like an elephant." Many birds eat up to 50% of their body weight each day. This describes the voracious manner in which leaders should learn. Elephants excrete a significant percentage of their body weight each day and then spread it around. Similarly, leaders should share what they have learned, to help others grow and develop. They should spread it around, just like an elephant. This example *elegantly* describes the next aspect of Factor 4, developing others.

## Interpersonal Dimension
### Developing Others
Harvey Firestone, founder of the tire company that bears his name, believed that "the growth and development of people is the highest calling of leadership." The same sentiment was echoed nearly 75 years later by Larry Bossidy, former Chairman and CEO of Honeywell and co-author of *Execution: The Discipline of Getting Things Done.* He declared emphatically that "nothing we do is more important than . . . developing people. At the end of the day you bet on people, not on strategies." Leaders do not just develop their own abilities. They also help others improve their knowledge and skills. This is what Kouzes and Posner call "enabling others to act," and it is one of the five exemplary practices of a leader.

As with the other factors, there is tremendous support for this concept from leadership authors and practitioners. Robin Sharma, author of *The Monk who Sold his Ferrari,* contends that "great leaders spend their days helping those around them manifest their highest human potential while they work towards a vision that adds value to the world at large." Sharma's words also illustrate the connection between Factor 3, *Inspiration,* and Factor 4, *Improvement.* Effective leaders recognize that followers make leadership powerful. Collaboration with followers is the only way to achieve the vision. Therefore, the success of the vision depends on the leader's ability to foster growth and development among followers.

Sharma goes on to state that "the greatest privilege of leadership is the chance to elevate lives." Similarly, Mark Sanborn declares that "leadership is an invitation to greatness." Leaders invite other people to become great and then facilitate the process. This is congruent with Factor 2, *Integrity*, which emphasizes the importance of caring as a way to build trust. One of the ways to show that you care is to sincerely commit to the improvement of those around you.

The importance of developing others is highlighted by the theories of servant leadership and stewardship. The theory of servant leadership, proposed by Robert Greenleaf, holds that the primary responsibility of a leader is to meet the needs of others and society. The purpose of leadership is not self-centered, it is others-centered. Similarly, the concept of stewardship, developed by Peter Block, implies that leaders are guardians of something which is not their own.

This attitude of service was clearly communicated by Dee Hock, founder and CEO Emeritus of Visa International. "If you don't understand that you work for your mislabeled 'subordinates,' then you know nothing of leadership." In Hock's view, subordinates are "mislabeled" because it is the leader who is subordinate. Max DePree refers to this as a state of indebtedness. Leaders subordinate themselves and are indebted to their followers. This is the opposite of most popular views of leadership.

Unfortunately, instead of helping others to "manifest their highest human potential," too many aspiring leaders simply use other people to achieve personal goals. This is exploitation and manipulation, not leadership. Similarly, some see followers as potential threats to their supremacy and deliberately attempt to thwart the success of their followers. I will discuss this in more detail in the section on Factor Fiction: Popularity, but first I will examine strategies for developing others.

There are many ways to develop those around you. This can be accomplished by sharing responsibility, involving others in decision making, giving challenging assignments, providing necessary resources, offering encouragement, promoting training opportunities, teaching and mentoring, incessant communication, rewarding failure, and succession planning.

### Sharing Responsibility

Some people believe that if you want something done right, you have to do it yourself. This belief limits many leaders' efforts to develop others. Development is not just a product of formal training. It also involves learning through experience. Followers improve their skills, abilities, and leadership potential when they have the opportunity to take on graduated levels of responsibility. As they demonstrate competence, they should be rewarded with even greater responsibilities. Ken Blanchard argued that successful followers are "in control of achieving the goal." By definition, if a leader *takes responsibility* for everything, then no one else has responsibility.

### Participation

Many leaders believe that they have the right to make all decisions and maybe they do. However, involving others in the decision-making process is an excellent way to help others grow. Leaders can encourage greater or lesser degrees of involvement based on the particular situation. At one extreme, leaders can delegate the research and final decision to an individual or group. At the other extreme, the leader can ask for input but reserve the right to make the final decision. Regardless of which method is chosen, effective leaders see each decision as an opportunity to contribute to the growth of those around them.

### Challenging Work

It is easy to delegate mundane and routine tasks. However, this only fosters a sense of insignificance among followers. Offering challenging work is similar to sharing responsibility and works on the same principle as action learning. Effectiveness requires both knowledge and skill. Furthermore, some things can only be learned through experience. For example, you cannot learn how to ride a bike by watching a video or listening to a speaker describe the process. Leaders must give others a chance to *ride the bike* if they hope to see them develop competence and confidence.

The value of challenging work has been recognized by both employees and employers. Many companies actually offer challenging tasks, instead of promotions, as a reward for successful performance. Similarly, like a successful photographer or architect, more and more employees see their work as an opportunity to build their portfolio of projects. Tom Peters is a strong advocate of this approach, which he refers

to as "Brand You." In an age where companies can no longer promise lifetime employment, successful employers offer to make people more employable. This is in contrast to the traditional goal of *climbing the corporate ladder*. Although, leadership is not necessarily tied to a corporate context, the same principle applies. Effective leaders help others to reach their potential, regardless of the purpose for which that potential is utilized. New challenges and meaningful assignments provide both motivation and opportunities to maximize one's potential.

### *Providing Resources*

One of my jobs involved developing a vocational rehabilitation program for nearly 200 adults with developmental disabilities. I had significant responsibilities, involvement in decisions, and a very challenging assignment. I was very excited to get started. When I arrived at work on the first day, one of my co-workers showed me to my new office. There was a desk, a chair, and a phone. One important piece of equipment was missing. There was no computer.

I was informed that there was a community computer lab with three computers. The lab was located in the middle of a busy office suite, and there was little space to set out my materials. When I needed to use a computer, it was necessary to sign up for a time on the schedule. This was very disheartening. It was 1997. The internet and email were a vital part of my daily work habits, but the company I worked for did not see the importance of providing these resources.

It is not enough to share responsibility, involve others in decision-making, and delegate challenging work. Leaders also need to procure the necessary resources to accomplish the goals of the group. If this does not happen, people become disillusioned.

### *Removing Barriers*

People attempting to achieve a worthwhile vision will inevitably encounter barriers to their progress. Leaders remove obstacles for their followers. This is one way that leaders can serve. Remember that people value leaders that are forward-looking. This means that leaders should, and often do, see problems before others. Effective leaders do whatever they can to ensure the progress of those around them. One way to do this is to antici-pate and provide the resources that people will need to accomplish the task.

### Providing Encouragement

Ken Blanchard writes that "cheering each other on" is essential to the achievement of any task. His books and speeches consistently focus on "catching others doing things right." This is the opposite of customary practice. Most leaders, especially in organizations, see it as their duty to find and point out the weaknesses of their followers. Unfortunately, as Dale Carnegie explained, people do not usually respond positively to criticism, and it often has the opposite effect.

"Encouraging the heart" is one of Kouzes and Posner's five exemplary practices of a leader. They believe that this practice is so important that they devoted an entire book to it. Encouragement means letting others know that they have what it takes to be successful. It means expressing confidence in their abilities and potential.

Mark Twain poignantly reinforced the relationship between leadership and encouragement when he wrote, "Keep away from people who belittle your ambitions. Small people always do that, but the really great make you feel that you too can become great." *Small* leaders derive their value from minimizing the worth of others. They believe that their greatness will be diminished by the accomplishments of others. On the other hand, *great* leaders recognize, acknowledge, and promote greatness in others. They do not have a need to feel better or superior. They have both the humility and self-confidence to recognize and praise the knowledge, abilities, and accomplishments of others.

This is important. Tom Morris argues that all successful people have a "strong confidence" in their ability to achieve the goal. Research on expectancy theory demonstrates that if people believe that they do not have the necessary skills, they will not attempt a task, regardless of the potential reward. Effective leaders help others to develop this confidence because they realize it is vital to the success of the shared vision. By offering encouragement, they literally *give courage*. This again reinforces the *me-first* principle. Leaders must have courage and confidence before they can give it to others.

### Promoting Learning

One way to promote learning is to devote yourself to learning. As was already discussed, your actions have a powerful influence on others. Leaders can also promote learning by providing the resources, including

time and money, for people to pursue education and training, formally and informally. The assignment of additional responsibilities and challenging work can be contingent on the level of competence that has been achieved. In this way, those who have demonstrated a commitment to learning are given greater opportunities to learn in new ways.

### Communicating Constantly

A leader is often a vital source of necessary information and knowledge. Because of this, it is very important for leaders to constantly and clearly communicate with followers. This is especially important as it relates to vision. It is probably impossible to overstate the importance of regular and comprehensive communication. This should involve use of every possible medium including: personal and group meetings, phone conversations, email, voice mail, personal notes, and formal memos. Again, the most powerful form of communication is the leader's behavior. All messages, verbal and behavioral, must be consistent.

### Rewarding Failure

Thomas Edison, one of the most famous inventors of all time, failed thousands of times before successfully developing a workable filament for the light bulb. His ability to overcome setbacks was based on his belief about failure. "I have not failed. I've just found 10,000 ways that won't work." He saw failure as a learning opportunity. It was not something to be avoided but, instead, rapidly pursued. Each failure ruled out one more possibility, thus narrowing down the options and bringing him closer to success. "I am not discouraged, because every wrong attempt discarded is another step forward."

In *Leading for Innovation,* Marshall Goldsmith wrote a chapter entitled "Why Smart People Can't Learn." In it, he explained that success often causes people to stop learning. Past successes lead to complacency, and the belief that what worked in the past will be sufficient for the future. In contrast, failure is a powerful teacher. Effective leaders are not afraid to fail, and they allow their followers to fail as well.

### Planning for Succession

An often quoted truth about leadership is that "there is no success without a successor." Effective leaders do not just develop followers, they develop leaders who eventually take their place. Ideally, succession planning is an intentional process and should be one of every leader's top

priorities. Walter Lippman argues that "The final test of a leader is that he leaves behind in others the conviction and will to carry on." In his "Law of Legacy," John Maxwell contends that "a leader's lasting value is measured by succession." The continued pursuit of the vision is dependent on a leader's ability to develop other leaders.

Ultimately, effective leaders not only nurture their successors but also, in the process of developing others, create leaders who pursue other visions or lead other organizations. John Maxwell called this the "Law of Reproduction." His research indicates that 85% of leaders credited their success to the "influence of another leader." This is reinforced by the following quote from Ralph Nader. "I start with the premise that the function of leadership is to produce more leaders, not more followers." The power of this principle was clearly illustrated in the opening story about Bill Walsh and is reinforced in the next section, which examines the career of Jack Welch.

### Factor Figure
#### *Jack Welch*
Jack Welch began working at General Electric (GE) in 1960. Twenty-one years later, he was the CEO. During his first five years, he was hardly known for his ability to develop others. In fact, he was widely despised for his decisions to layoff thousands of workers and close many of GE's businesses. However, by the time he retired in 2001, these feelings had changed dramatically. The reasons for the change were evident even after he stepped down.

He was succeeded by Jeffrey Immelt, whom he had personally selected for the job. Immelt, who had been CEO of GE Medical Systems, was a product of Welch's tremendous focus on leadership development. Robert Nardelli and James McNerney were also internal candidates for the position but were not selected. However, when they were passed over for the CEO slot, Nardelli was immediately hired as the head of Home Depot and McNerney was brought on as chief executive of 3M.

Many other CEOs of Fortune 500 companies also come from GE. Welch was so good at developing leaders that his company did not have room to allow them all to achieve their potential. As a result, GE is recognized as one of the best companies to work for in America. Top

candidates from around the world compete for positions in various GE businesses.

While running GE, Welch spent at least 50% of his time on leadership development. Because of this focus, his company had, and continues to have, one of the most sophisticated processes for evaluating, developing, and promoting leaders. When a person is promoted, the vacancy created is filled within twenty-four hours, and each subsequent vacancy is also filled in that same time period. GE already knows who is ready for the next assignment before jobs become available.

Additionally, Welch created a training program that became the model for every business in America. Before becoming professor of organizational behavior at the University of Michigan, Noel Tichy was in charge of GE's Crotonville training site. It was there that he pioneered the process of action learning mentioned earlier in the chapter. The facilities, faculty, and curriculum reflected Welch's dedication to learning, training, and growth.

Welch was also a proponent of *dialogue* and *workout*. *Dialogue* was used in meetings and required participants to ask and answer the most important questions about business operations and individual performance. It demanded that everyone in the room be honest and give real feedback to each other. This is contrasted with most corporate meetings that involve various people giving reports while others sit and listen. Dialogue engaged everyone in the process of learning each day. GE employees were constantly receiving feedback about their performance and given opportunities to make the necessary improvements.

*Workout* was a process designed to take unnecessary work out of people's jobs. Over the course of a few days, employees would meet in both large and small groups to discuss ways to improve efficiency and effectiveness in their departments. The rules stated that each manager must respond to the ideas that were generated in a specific amount of time. Thousands of these ideas were implemented over the years, leading to millions of dollars in savings for the company.

Welch is a great example of improvement because he demonstrated so many different facets of leadership development. He promoted formal training, informal learning, succession planning, employee

involvement, participation in decision-making, and the removal of barriers. Many leaders neglect these processes because they fear the loss of their followers to other organizations or causes, or the loss of their own position. However, as Welch demonstrated, a reputation for leadership development only serves to attract even more qualified leadership candidates. Furthermore, it is interesting to note that Welch's relentless focus on the growth of others ultimately led to tremendous personal success and fame.

## Factor Failure
### *"Chainsaw" Al Dunlap*

"Chainsaw" Al Dunlap is the former CEO of Scott Paper and Sunbeam. He earned his nickname for the way he cut jobs, closed plants, doctored financial statements, and duped investors. Brought in to *turnaround* troubled companies, he actually destroyed them. He sacrificed the overall health of the company for superficial short-term returns that benefited him and a select group of inside investors. In the process, he was the subject of numerous interviews, high-profile articles, and other media attention. Wall Street loved him. He became a celebrity, but he was not an effective leader.

A recent *Fast Company* article featured Dunlap in a discussion of "psychopathic" bosses. New research demonstrates that many famous CEOs display traits associated with psychopathic personality disorder. "Chainsaw" Al was one of those CEOs. "The psychopathic boss doesn't understand that the job of leadership is to fully utilize human potential, to create organizations in which people can grow and learn while still achieving a common objective, to nurture the human spirit. This leader is devoted to self and self alone."

"Dunlap sucked the very life and soul out of companies and people" to feed his own desire for celebrity and fame, and it seemed to work. Jim Collins pointed out that, despite Dunlap's failures, he graced the covers of the most prestigious business publications. In contrast, Darwin Smith, who engineered a long-lasting turnaround of Kimberly Clark, is virtually unknown.

Smith is one the best examples in the twentieth century of a leader taking a company from merely good to truly great. And yet few people—even ardent students of business history—have heard of Darwin Smith. He probably would have liked it that way. Smith is

a classic example of what we have come to call a *Level 5 leader*—an individual who blends extreme personal humility with intense professional will."

Collins found that the leaders of great companies were focused on what they could "build, create and contribute." In contrast, mediocre companies were led by men who only pursued "fame, fortune, adulation, power." Leaders who subscribe to the myth of popularity are "concerned more with their own reputation for personal greatness" than they are with "setting the company up for success in the next generation."

## Factor Fiction
### *Popularity*

Instead of focusing on personal improvement and the development of others, many people seem to equate fame with leadership. They are focused on promoting their own celebrity rather than helping others reach their potential. This is problematic for four reasons. First, as with the idea of power, this view eliminates most people from leadership. Most people will not be famous. They will not be featured on television or in popular magazines.

Second, as was discussed in previous factors, effective leaders are not exclusively focused on self. They genuinely care for others, which is an important part of *Integrity*, and they are pursuing a shared vision that extends beyond their own interests, which is essential for *Inspiration*. Celebrity puts the spotlight on the individual leader, instead of a worthwhile vision.

Third, simply achieving popularity says nothing about one's ability to lead. In fact, Jim Collins, author of *Built to Last* and *Good to Great*, argued that, over the long-term, "celebrity is inversely correlated with leadership success." His research demonstrated that Level 5 leaders actually shunned the limelight, even when their success created opportunities for fame.

In contrast, ineffective leaders' pursuit of publicity actually detracted from the success of their organizations. Additionally, Kouzes and Posner's research showed that parents, coaches, and teachers are those with the most impact on people's lives. Famous people are not the most

influential leaders. Many times, their celebrity only serves to disguise their ineffectiveness as a leader.

Fourth, achieving celebrity tempts many leaders to take credit away from followers. To enhance their stature, they often actively suppress others' potential. Because the success of others is a threat to their supremacy, they do not want anyone else in the headlines.

Unfortunately, the relationship between celebrity and leadership has its roots in reality. Some effective leaders, like Jack Welch, do achieve a certain level of fame or celebrity. However, this is often the *result* of their leadership effectiveness, not the *cause*. Many people confuse this result with the origins of leadership success.

Al Dunlap is one example of the pursuit of popularity at the expense of true leadership. However, effective leaders are dedicated to learning and personal growth. They also share their knowledge and experiences with others. Their commitment to helping others improve distinguishes them from leaders whose only focus is personal popularity.

> If you'd like to learn more about how to improve your leadership, go to www.drendall.com and order GROW! Ten Strategies for Maximizing your Leadership Potential. Available in 60-minute Audio CD or DVD.

**Factor Focus**
1. Do you have a personal development plan?
2. What is your learning style?
   a. Visual
   b. Auditory
   c. Kinesthetic
3. What is the next step in your leadership development?
4. Who would you like have as a mentor? How could you initiate that relationship?
5. What would you do with an hour of time for personal renewal?
6. How could you build on your existing strengths?
7. What barriers could you remove for your followers?
8. What resources do your followers need?
9. How could you increase the level of participation in your team?

10. Do you provide challenging opportunities to others? Why or why not?
11. What is a challenge that you could delegate?
12. How could you encourage someone?
13. Do you know a person who would benefit from having a mentor? How could you initiate that relationship?
14. What kind of people would complement your strengths?
15. What could you do to begin developing your successor?
16. Collins says that "celebrity is inversely correlated with leadership." If this is true, then why do so many people pursue popularity?
17. What have others done to "belittle your ambitions?"
18. How can you invite other people to become great?

### Factor Future
1. Create a personal development plan.
2. Take a class.
3. Attend a seminar.
4. Take a trip.
5. Try to fail.
6. Take time for personal renewal.
7. Sign up for Audible.com
8. Start a journal.
9. Become a mentor.
10. Find a mentor.
11. Read selected books from the factor facts section.
12. Create a leadership development program for your organization.
13. Encourage someone.
14. Develop systems that promote regular communication with your followers.
15. Identify the resources that your people need to complete their work.
16. Quit your job and join a company that has tuition reimbursement.

### Factor Facts

Kouzes & Posner *A Leader's Legacy*

Loehr & Schwartz *The Power of Full Engagement*

http://www.cbass.com/Intervalsforlife.htm
- Online article with a great overview of Loehr & Schwartz's book

Maxwell                    *Failing Forward*
- Excellent argument for the importance of failure.

Maxwell                    *Developing the Leaders Around You*

## Factor Finder

*Learning Style*
http://www.learning-styles-online.com/inventory/questions.asp
Requires a short registration process, which also subscribes you to a
newsletter. You can unsubscribe if you don't want it.
Site provides a good overview of seven different learning styles.

http://www.mindtools.com/mnemlsty.html
Good one page review of three dominant learning styles.

http://www.nwlink.com/~donclark/hrd/learning/styles.html
Excellent resource. Provides suggestions for responding to people's
particular learning style, as well as an overview of the concept of multiple
intelligences.

http://adulted.about.com/gi/dynamic/offsite.htm?zi=1/XJ&sdn=adulted&zu
=http%3A%2F%2Fwww.engr.ncsu.edu%2Flearningstyles%2Filsweb.html
Offers good explanation of each style type. Seems similar to personality
style.

*Leadership Practices Inventory*
http://www.lpionline.com/lpi/
Based on Kouzes and Posner's Leadership Challenge
(requires survey administration and purchase of license)
- *Enable Others to Act*

*21 Irrefutable Laws of Leadership*
http://www.injoy.com/OnlineTools/assessment.aspx
Based on John Maxwell's book with the same title
21 different assessments for each leadership law
Requires free, brief online registration (email address, name, zipcode)
- *Inner Circle: A leader's potential is determined by those closest to him*
- *Empowerment: Only secure leaders give power to others*
- *Reproduction: It takes a leader to raise up a leader*

*- Explosive Growth: To add growth, lead followers – To multiply, lead leaders*
*- Legacy: The leader's lasting value is measured by succession*

*17 Indisputable Laws of Teamwork*
http://www.injoy.com/OnlineTools/assessment.aspx
Based on John Maxwell's book with the same title
17 different assessments for each teamwork law
Requires free, brief online registration (email address, name, zipcode)
*- Dividends: Investing in the team compounds over time*
*- Bench: Great teams have great depth*
*- Significance: One is too small a number to achieve greatness*
*- Mount Everest: As the challenges escalates, the need for teamwork elevates*

---

If you know about other interesting resources, self-assessments, or application ideas, please send an email to me at dave@drendall.com I'd love to add your submission to the four factors resources on my website www.drendall.com and/or to future editions of the book.

---

### Factor Foundation

| | |
|---|---|
| **Bass** *Leadership and Performance Beyond Expectation* <br><br> **Burns** *Leadership* | Transformational Leadership <br> - Intellectual Stimulation |
| **Covey** *The Seven Habits of Highly Effective People* | Seven Habits <br> - Habit 4: Think Win-Win <br> - Habit 6: Synergize <br> - Habit 7: Sharpen the Saw |
| **Collins** *Good to Great* | Level 5 Leadership <br> - Level 5: Extreme Humility & Intense Will |
| **Finzel** *The Top Ten Mistakes Leaders Make* | Top Ten Mistakes <br> - Success without Successors <br> - Dirty Delegation |

| Kouzes & Posner<br>*The Leadership Challenge* | Five Exemplary Practices<br>- Enable Others to Act |
|---|---|
| **Maxwell**<br>*The 21 Irrefutable Laws of Leadership* | 21 Irrefutable Laws<br>- Inner Circle: A leader's potential is determined by those closest to him<br>- Empowerment: Only secure leaders give power to others<br>- Reproduction: It takes a leader to raise up a leader<br>- Explosive Growth: To add growth, lead followers – To multiply, lead leaders<br>- Legacy: The leader's lasting value is measured by succession |
| *The 21 Indispensable Qualities of a Leader* | 21 Indispensable Qualities<br>- Generosity: Your candle loses nothing when it lights another<br>- Servanthood: To get ahead, put others first<br>- Teachability: To keep leading, keep learning |
| **Senge**<br>*The Fifth Discipline* | Five Disciplines<br>- Team Learning<br>- Systems Thinking<br><br>Learning Organizations |

## Factor Quotient
### *Improvement*

Please read each of the statements listed below.
Record your level of agreement with each statement in the blank to the left.
Total your answers and refer to the scoring key at the end of the assessment.

*5 Strongly Agree    4 Agree    3 Not Sure    2 Disagree    1 Strongly Disagree*

---

_____  1. I have a *mentor* with whom I regularly meet.
_____  2. I frequently *read* books, magazines, and websites.
_____  3. I am a good *listener*.
_____  4. I examine my *paradigms*, the lenses I use to see the world.
_____  5. I consistently seek out *new experiences*.
_____  6. I *teach* others.
_____  7. I *encourage* others.
_____  8. I *share responsibility* and involve others in *decision-making*.
_____  9. I serve as a *mentor* for others.
_____  10. I see *failure* as an opportunity to learn. I allow others to fail.

_____  **Total Score**

**Scoring Key**
**41-50**   Great, maximize your abilities in this factor
**31-40**   Good, continue to fine-tune certain aspects of this factor
**21-30**   You may want to focus attention on this factor
**< 26**    This factor might be a barrier to your leadership effectiveness

# Impact

Never doubt that a small group of thoughtful, concerned citizens can change world. Indeed it is the only thing that ever has.

- Margaret Mead

### A New Definition

In chapter 1, I used Drucker's definition, that leadership is having followers, as a starting point for examining the nature of effective leadership. Since then, I have clarified this definition and added to it. The me-first principle demonstrated that *leadership begins with you*. To be a leader of others, you must first master yourself. This principle was woven throughout the book as each factor included an area for personal development. Effective leaders have self-discipline, credibility, a sense of personal mission and a commitment to self-improvement. Leadership begins with you, but it does not end there.

Factors 1 and 2 showed that *leadership is a relationship*. As Drucker said, it requires followers. Leadership is not a solitary activity. It requires *Influence* with others and the trust that comes from *Integrity*. However, leadership is not just a relationship.

Factors 3 contended that this relationship requires a direction. Personal mission and shared vision offer *Inspiration* and provide a focal point for the interaction between leaders and followers. Factor 4 argued that this relationship also needs to include the *Improvement* of both leaders and followers. It should be mutually beneficial.

Leadership is not found in the pursuit of power, personality, position, or popularity because these goals are in direct opposition to the four factors of effective leadership. The use of *power* diminishes *influence*. Reliance on superficial *personality* undermines *integrity*. Dependence on *position* and authority neglects the *inspirational* value of vision. A desire for *popularity* causes people to diminish the value of others instead of helping them to *improve*.

The following poem provides a clear contrast between the factors of effective leadership and each element of factor fiction. I divided the poem into sections that correlate with the four factors.

Are you a boss or a leader? Rate yourself on the standards in this poem attribute to H. Gordon Selfridge:

*Factor 1: Influence vs. Power*
The boss drives people; the leader coaches them.
The boss says "Get here on time;" the leader gets there ahead of time.
The boss commands; the leader asks.
The boss never has enough time; the leader has time for things that count.

*Factor 2: Integrity vs. Personality*
The boss says "Go;" the leader says "Let's go."
The boss is concerned with things; the leader is concerned with people.

*Factor 3: Inspiration vs. Position*
The boss depends on authority; the leader on goodwill.
The boss inspires fear; the leader inspires enthusiasm.
The boss sees today; the leader also looks at tomorrow.

*Factor 4: Improvement vs. Popularity*
The boss says "I;" the leader says "We."
The boss fixes the blame for the breakdown; the leader fixes the breakdown.
The boss knows how it is done; the leader shows how.
The boss uses people; the leader develops them.
The boss lets a person know where she stands; the leader lets people know where they stand.
The boss works hard to produce; the leader works hard to help his people produce.
The boss takes the credit; the leader gives it.

Ultimately, I believe that leadership can be defined as a *relationship that produces positive change.* Factors 1 and 2 showed you how to develop that relationship. Factors 3 focused on positive changes in

the world, and Factor 4 illustrated strategies for improving yourself and others. Therefore, *leadership is a relationship that produces positive change in self, others, and the world*. Leadership is ultimately about results. It is about making an impact first in your own life, then in the lives of those around you, and finally in the broader community and the world.

In this final chapter I want to focus on two aspects of this definition, the words *positive* and *change*. Remember your life will make a difference. The only remaining question is what kind of difference it will make. Not all change is positive. However, any growth or improvement does require change.

### Change

Kouzes and Posner believe that leaders "challenge the process." Leaders are not satisfied with current reality. They want to create change. This was the essence of James McGregor Burns' concept of transformational leadership. Leaders transform themselves, others, and the world around them. Similarly, Joseph Rost, in *Leadership in the 21st Century*, argues that leaders and followers must "intend real changes." John Maxwell wrote that "creating positive change is the ultimate test of leadership." The following quote from Theodore Roosevelt, eloquently communicates the rationale and reward for pursuing change.

> It is not the critic who counts: not the man who points out how the strong man stumbles or where the doer of deeds could have done better. The credit belongs to the man who is actually in the arena, whose face is marred by dust and sweat and blood, who strives valiantly, who errs and comes up short again and again, because there is no effort without error or shortcoming, but who knows the great enthusiasms, the great devotions, *who spends himself for a worthy cause*; who, at the best, knows, in the end, the triumph of high achievement, and who, at the worst, if he fails, at least he fails while daring greatly, so that his place shall never be with those cold and timid souls who knew neither victory nor defeat.

### Positive

If Roosevelt is right, then what is a worthy cause? What do I mean by positive change? The word *positive* is important because some people believe that effective leadership can be exercised in the process of creating negative change. This is why Hitler, Machiavelli, and Tony Soprano are

often cited as effective leaders. I have attempted to demonstrate the inadequacy of this perspective through the Factor Fiction sections in each chapter.

Furthermore, negative purposes seem to bear within themselves the seeds of their own undoing. Ralph Waldo Emerson, in his classic evaluation of Napoleon Bonaparte, explained the dictator's eventual failure this way.

> It was not Bonaparte's fault. He did all that in him lay to live and thrive *without moral principle*. It was the nature of things, the eternal law of man and of the world which baulked and ruined him; and the result, in a million experiments, will be the same. Every experiment, by multitudes or by individuals, that has a *sensual* and *selfish aim*, will *fail*. . . Only that good profits which we can taste with all doors open, and which *serves all men*.

### Serving Others

The ultimate definition of what constitutes positive change is certainly problematic, and I won't propose a comprehensive definition. However, Emerson provided a perspective which many people share. Positive changes are those which serve "all men." Emerson believed that only leaders who pursued positive changes could succeed. Negative changes, those with "sensual and selfish" aims, will always fail.

It seems that positive changes involve being focused on the needs of others, instead of exclusively on self-interest. Leaders do focus on self, on *me-first,* but only as a means to produce positive changes in others and the world. They put on their oxygen mask so that they can help others.

For example, one of Covey's seven habits is "sharpen the saw." In his analogy, self is the saw, the tool through which you accomplish your goals. You must regularly sharpen, or improve, yourself in order to have a positive impact on others. The focus on self must ultimately be augmented by a broader interest in the needs of others and the world.

Some notable historical figures reinforce the importance of a focus on others. Helen Keller contended that "many people have a wrong idea of what constitutes true happiness. It is not attained through *self-gratification*, but through fidelity to a *worthy purpose*." Positive changes are "worthy" purposes; Keller contrasted them with "self-gratification."

Philosopher and popular author George Bernard Shaw supported Keller's view.

> This is the true joy in life, the *being used up for a purpose recognized by yourself as a mighty one*, the being a force of nature, instead of a feverish, *selfish*, little clod of ailments and grievances complaining that the world will not devote itself to making you happy. I am of the opinion, that *my life belongs to the whole community*, and as long as I live, it is my privilege to do for it whatever I can. I want to be thoroughly used up when I die, for the harder I work the more I live. I rejoice in life for its own sake. Life is no brief candle to me. It is a sort of splendid torch, which I've got to hold up for the moment and I want to make it burn as brightly as possible before *handing it on to future generations*.

Again, "mighty" purposes are juxtaposed with "selfish" concerns. Shaw believed that his life belonged "to the whole community." This echoes the theory of servant leadership and DePree's conception of leadership as indebtedness.

### Enduring Change

I believe that positive changes are also long-term changes. Consider Shaw's concern for "future generations." Short-term results do not require effective leadership, and they often disguise the ultimate futility of pursuing negative purposes. The lives of Hitler, Jim Jones, Napoleon, and, to a lesser degree, "Chainsaw" Al Dunlap illustrate this point. They were briefly admired, revered, and emulated, but their lasting legacy was one of failure. Momentary accomplishment can be achieved through inappropriate means and ends. However, this seeming success cannot be sustained. Effective leaders recognize that positive changes are those that endure.

In *The Emperor's Club,* a movie that followed the lives of a boarding school teacher and his students, Kevin Kline's character tried to challenge his class to pursue truly positive changes. He told the story of past rulers who were once famous and powerful but were now almost unknown. In his conclusion, he clearly stated his point and asked two related and penetrating questions. "Great ambition and conquest, without contribution, are without significance. What will your contribution be? How will history remember you?" I would encourage you to consider these two questions as

well. Leadership cannot be separated from a desire for enduring changes focused on the welfare of others. That is what I mean by positive change.

## Final Challenge

I would like to leave you with one final challenge. As you reflect on what you have read in this book, remember that *leadership begins with you*. If this is true, then leadership development can start right now. Leadership is not a position, so you do not have to wait until you get promoted to a formal leadership position. It is not popularity, so you do not have to wait until you are discovered by the media. You can get started right away. I would encourage you to begin right now. In the words of John Gardner "The cynic says 'one man can't do anything.' I say 'only one man can do anything.'" The lives of Wild Bill Holden, Markita, Melissa, and Tommy demonstrate the truth of these words.

This book can serve as a road map for your leadership development. You can use the assessments at the end of each chapter to evaluate your areas of strength and areas for improvement. I would recommend the following process. Start with the internal dimension of Factor 1, Self-discipline. Ask yourself, do I have self-discipline or is this a major challenge for me? If it is an area in which you struggle, stop there and explore strategies for improving your self-discipline.

If you can honestly say that you consistently demonstrate self-discipline, if you regularly delay gratification and wait for the second marshmallow, then move on to the interpersonal facet of Factor 1, Influence. Ask yourself, do I have influence in my relationships with others? If, despite your self-discipline, you have difficulty influencing others, then begin to develop methods for expanding your influence. Each factor builds on the foundation of the one before it. Although no one will ever have complete mastery of each factor, efforts to improve in the competencies of later factors will be hampered by any significant weaknesses in earlier factors.

Finally, as Mark Sanborn says, I believe that "truth is transferable." In other words, the factors of effective leadership can also be applied to other areas of your life. These factors apply to successful teaching, parenting, marriage, organizations, and any other relationship in which you would like to produce positive change. As I have studied psychology, counseling, and leadership throughout the years, I have noticed

tremendous similarities in the advice of marital therapists, parenting experts, education researchers, and management and leadership gurus. The four factors are my attempt to assemble all of this wisdom in one place.

I would encourage you to begin practicing the four factors with your children, spouse, co-workers, bosses, or students. If leadership is a relationship that produces positive change, then opportunities to exercise effective leadership are all around you. I wish you success on your leadership journey.

### Factor Focus
1. What are the most important relationships in your life?
2. Are your goals focused on selfish interests or the needs of others?
3. What are you doing that will have an enduring impact?
4. What can you do today to begin improving your effectiveness as a leader?

### Factor Future
1. List three relationships in which you would like to create positive change.
2. Choose at least one action step from the four factors to begin improving each relationship.
3. Send me an email to dave@drendall.com and subscribe to the weekly *Four Factors Follow-Up* email, which includes quotes from the book, application ideas and other resources for improving your leadership.
4. Send me an email to let me know how you are changing the world.

### Factor Facts
| | |
|---|---|
| Covey | *The Eighth Habit* |
| Kotter | *Leading Change* |
| O'Toole | *Leading Change* |

# About the Author

David Rendall is an international speaker, author, and consultant. He is principal and founder of Rendall & Associates, a consulting firm dedicated to developing leaders in business and nonprofit organizations. He has provided training and consulting services to people and organizations throughout the United States, Canada, Australia and the United Kingdom.

He is currently Assistant Professor of Business at Mount Olive College and was nominated for Teacher of the Year in 2006. He has taught graduate and undergraduate courses in leadership, innovation, strategic management, organizational change, and psychology for Judson College, University of Phoenix, Keller Graduate School of Management and Trinity Western University. He also presents seminars for Duke University's certificate program in nonprofit management and advanced certificate in nonprofit leadership.

Prior to becoming a professor and consultant, he developed and managed nonprofit enterprises that provided employment for people with disabilities. He has more than ten years of experience leading people and organizations.

He earned a doctor of management degree in organizational leadership from the University of Phoenix. He has a graduate degree in counseling psychology from the University of Wisconsin - Milwaukee and an undergraduate degree in psychology from Judson College.

This is his first book. His previous work as an author includes articles and book reviews related to marketing, knowledge management, personal development and social enterprise.

To learn more about Rendall & Associates please contact Dave or visit one of the sites below.

phone:   (919) 222-6295
email:    dave@drendall.com

web:     www.drendall.com
blog:    www.daverendall.typepad.com
lens:    www.squidoo.com/rendall

# References

a Kempis, T. (1998). *The imitation of Christ*. New York: Vintage.

Ambrose, S. (1998). Citizen soldiers. New York: Simon & Schuster.

Andrews, M. (1986). *How to sell more cookies, condos, Cadillacs, computers . . . and everything else*. New York: Vintage.

Aurelius, M. (2002). *Meditations*. New York: Modern Library.

Bass, B. (1990). *Bass & Stogdill's handbook of leadership* (3rd ed.). New York: Free Press.

Beecher, H. W. http://www.leadershipnow.com/disciplinequotes.html

Bennis, W. (1989). *On becoming a leader.* Reading, Massachusetts: Addison-Wesley.

Bennis, W. & Goldsmith, J. (1997). *Learning to lead.* Reading, Massachusetts: Perseus Books.

Bennis, W. & Nanus, B. (1985). *Leaders.* New York: Harper Perennial.

Blanchard, K. & Johnson, S. (1981). *The one-minute manager*. New York: Berkley.

Blanchard, K. (1998). *Gung Ho!* New York: William Morrow and Company.

Block, P. (1993). *Stewardship*. San Francisco: Berrett-Koehler.

Bolman, L. & Deal, T. (1997). *Reframing organizations* (2nd Ed.). San Francisco: Jossey-Bass.

Bossidy, L. & Charan, R. (2002). *Execution: The discipline of getting things done.* New York: Crown Business.

Burns, J. (1982). *Leadership*. New York: Harper Perennial.

Byrne, J. (2005, July). Working for the boss from hell. *Fast Company,* p. 14.

Canfield, J. (2005). *The success principles*. New York: Harper Collins.

Canfield, J. & Hansen, M. (1993). *Chicken soup for the soul*. Deerfield Beach, Florida: Health Communications.

Carnegie, D. (1974). *How to win friends and influence people*. New York: Pocket Books.

Carroll, L. (1971). *Alice's adventures in wonderland*. New York: W. W. Norton.

Cartwright (Ed.), *Studies in social power* (pp. 150-167). Ann Arbor, Michigan: Institute for Social Research.

Charan, R. & Tichy, N. (2000). *Every business is a growth business*. Pittsburgh: Three Rivers Press.

Cialdini, R. (1993). *Influence: Science and practice* (3$^{rd}$ Ed.). New York: Harper Collins College Publishers.

Collins, J. & Porras, J. (1994). *Built to last*. New York: Harper Business.

Collins, J. (2001). *Good to great*. New York: Harper Business.

Covey, S. (1989). *The seven habits of highly effective people*. New York: Fireside.

Covey, S. (1990). *Principle-centered leadership*. New York: Fireside.

Covey, S. (1996). Three roles of the leader in the new paradigm. In F. Hesselbein, M. Goldsmith, & R. Beckhard (Eds), *The leader of the future* (pp. 149-159). San Francisco: Jossey-Bass Publishers.

Covey, S. (2005). *The eighth habit*. New York: Free Press.

Covey, S., Merrill, A., & Merrill, R. (1994). *First things first*. New York: Fireside.

DeGrosky, M. (2004). When leaders become followers.
http://wildfiremag.com/ar/leaders_become_followers/

DePree, M. (1989). *Leadership is an art.* New York: Doubleday.

DePree, M. (1992). *Leadership jazz.* New York: Dell Publishing.

DePree, M. (1997). *Leading without power.* San Francisco: Jossey-Bass.

Deutschman, A. (2005, July). Is your boss a psychopath? *Fast Company,* p.
44-51.

Drucker, P. (1966). *The effective executive.* New York: Harper Business.

Drucker, P. (1973). *Management.* New York: Harper & Row, Publishers.

Drucker, P. (1990). *Managing the nonprofit organization.* New York:
Harper Collins Publishers.

Emerson, R. (1947). *Napoleon.* Indiana University.

Epictetus. quoted in Morris, T. (1994)

Finzel, H. (1994). *The top ten mistakes leaders make.* Colorado Springs,
Colorado: Victor Books.

Frankl, V. (1963). *Man's search for meaning.* New York: Pocket Books.

French, J. & Raven, B. (1959). The bases of social power. In D. P.

Fuller, G. ( 1991). *How to learn a foreign language.* New York: Storm King
Press.

Gardner, J. (1987). Leaders and followers. In J. T. Wren (Ed.), *The leader's*
companion: Insights on leadership through the ages (pp.
185-188). New York: Free Press.

Gardner, J. (1990). *On leadership.* New York: Free Press.

Goleman, D. (1995). *Emotional intelligence.* New York: Bantam Books

Goleman, D. (1998). *Working with emotional intelligence.* New York: Bantam Books.

Goleman, D., McKee, A. & Boyatzis, R. (2002). *Primal leadership.* Boston, Massachusetts: Harvard Business School Press.

Greenleaf, R. (1977). *Servant leadership.* New York: Paulist Press.

Griffin, R. (2005). *Management* (8th Ed.). New York: Houghton Miflin Company.

Helweg-Larsen, M. & Collins, B. (1997, April). A social psychological perspective on the role of knowledge about AIDS in AIDS prevention. *Current Directions in Psychological Science,* pp. 23-26.

Hesselbein, F. (2002). *Hesselbein on leadership.* San Francisco: Jossey-Bass.

Hesselbein, F., Goldsmith, M., & Beckhard, R. (Eds). (1996). *The leader of the future.* San Francisco: Jossey-Bass Publishers.

Hock, D. (1999). *Birth of the chaordic age.* New York: Berrett-Koehler.

Holden, Bill
http://sports.espn.go.com/espn/page2/story?page=drehs/050606

Kawasaki, G. (2000). *Rules for revolutionaries.* New York: Collins.

Kelley, R. (1988). In praise of followers. In J. T. Wren (Ed.), *The leader's companion: Insights on leadership through the ages* (pp. 193-204). New York: Free Press.

Kotter, J. (1990). What leaders really do. In J. Wren (Ed.). *The leader's companion: Insights on leadership through the ages* (pp. 114-124). New York: Free Press.

Kotter, J. (1996). *Leading Change.* Boston, Massachusetts: Harvard Business School Press.

Kouzes, J. & Posner, B. (2003). *The leadership challenge*. San Francisco: Jossey-Bass.

Kouzes, J. & Posner. B. (1999). *Encouraging the heart*. San Francisco: Jossey-Bass.

Kouzes, J. & Posner, B. (1993). *Credibility*. San Francisco: Jossey-Bass.

Krzyzewski, M. (2001). *Leading with the heart*. New York: Warner Business Books.

Lao Tzu. (1963). *Tao te ching*. New York: Penguin Books.

Lencioni, P. (1998). *The five temptations of a CEO*. San Francisco: Jossey-Bass.

Loehr, J & Schwartz, T. (2003). *The power of full engagement*. New York: Free Press.

Machiavelli, N. (1981). *The prince*. London: Penguin Books.

Manz, C. & Neck, C, (1998) Mastering self leadership (2nd Ed.). New York: Prentice Hall.

Maxwell, J. (1993). *Developing the leader within you*. Nashville: Thomas Nelson Publishers.

Maxwell, J. (1997). *Developing the leaders around you*. Nashville: Thomas Nelson Publishers.

Maxwell, J. (1998). *The 21 irrefutable laws of leadership*. Nashville: Thomas Nelson Publishers.

McCullough, D. (2005). *1776*. New York: Simon & Schuster.

Morris, T. (1994). *True success*. New York: G. P. Putnam's Sons.

Myers, D. (2002). *Social psychology* (7th Ed.). Boston: McGraw Hill.

Nanda, B. (1965). *Mahatma Gandhi*. Woodbury, New York: Barron's.

O'Toole, J. (1996). *Leading change: The argument for value based leadership*. New York: Ballantine Books.

Peters, T. (1999). *Reinventing work: The brand you 50*. New York: Alfred A. Knopf.

Pink, D. (2005). *A whole new mind: Why right-brainers will rule future*. New York: Riverhead Books.

Plato, quoted in Morris, T. (1994).

Pollard, C. (1996). *The soul of the firm*. New York: Harper Business.

Quinn, R. (1996). *Deep change: Discovering the leader within*. San Francisco: Jossey-Bass.

Reuter, quoted in Rost, J. (1993).

Rost, J. (1993). *Leadership for the 21$^{st}$ century*. New York: Praeger.

Rotter, J. (1966). Generalized expectancies for internal versus external control of reinforcements, *Psychological Monographs, 80,* Whole No. 609.

Sanborn, M. (2004). *The fred factor*. Colorado Springs, Colorado: Waterbrook Press.

Schein, E. (1996). Leadership and organizational culture. In F. Hesselbein, M. Goldsmith, & R. Beckhard (Eds), *The leader of the future* (pp. 59-70). San Francisco: Jossey-Bass Publishers.

Selfridge, H. G. http://www.quotationsbook.com/quotes/22941/view

Senge, P. (1990). *The fifth discipline*. New York: Doubleday Currency.

Severe, S. (2003). *How to behave so your children will too*. New York: Penguin Books.

Sharma, R. (1999). *The monk who sold his Ferrari*. San Francisco: Harper San Francisco

Stanley, A. (1999). *Visioneering.* Sisters, Oregon: Multnomah.

Stevenson, R. L. (2002). *The strange case of Dr. Jekyll and Mr. Hyde.* New York: W. W. Norton.

Swindoll, C. http://www.bigeye.com/attitude.htm

Welch, J. (2001). *Jack: Straight from the gut.* New York: Warner Business Books.

Wilde, O. (1998). *The picture of Dorian Gray.* New York: Modern Library.

Wistrich, R. (1997). *Who's who in Nazi Germany.* New York: Routledge.

Ziglar, Z. (2002). *A view from the top.* New York: Simon & Schuster Audio.

1890251

Made in the USA